STARTING A STARTUP

JAMES SINCLAIR

STARTING A STARTUP
BUILD SOMETHING PEOPLE WANT

Copyright © 2025 by James Sinclair

All rights reserved. No part of this book may be reproduced, stored in a retrieval system or transmitted, in any form or by any means, without the prior written consent of the publisher or a license from The Canadian Copyright Licensing Agency (Access Copyright). For a copyright license, visit accesscopyright.ca or call toll free to 1-800-893-5777.

Cataloguing in publication information is available from Library and Archives Canada.
ISBN 978-1-77458-639-6 (paperback)
ISBN 978-1-77458-681-5 (ebook)

Page Two
pagetwo.com

Page Two™ is a trademark owned by Page Two Strategies Inc., and is used under license by authorized licensees

Cover design by Peter Cocking
Interior design by Cameron McKague
Printed and bound in Canada by Friesens
Distributed in Canada by Raincoast Books
Distributed in the US and internationally by Macmillan

25 26 27 28 29   5 4 3 2 1

startuptoscaleup.com

CONTENTS

Introduction *1*

PART ONE MYTHS, MISINFORMATION, AND MOTIVATION

1. Let's Fucking Go *11*
2. Get Ready for AI *33*

PART TWO THE EARN THE RIGHT FRAMEWORK

3. Earn the Right to Solve a Problem, Part 1 *45*
4. Earn the Right to Solve a Problem, Part 2 *63*
5. Earn the Right to Enter the Market *75*
6. Earn the Right to Avoid Chasing Product-Market Fit *101*
7. Earn the Right to Build Something *115*
8. Earn the Right to Delight *139*
9. Earn the Right to Ship *157*
10. Earn the Right to Grow *175*
11. Earn the Right to (Not) Launch *185*
12. Earn the Right to Sell *197*
13. Earn the Right to (Not) Pivot *221*
14. Earn the Right to AI, Part 2 *237*
15. Earn the Right to Take a Vacation *249*

Acknowledgments *253*

Notes *255*

INTRODUCTION

BUILD A WINNING TEAM, create something people want and are willing to pay for, do it fast, keep it lean. That's the whole playbook.

Welcome, first-time founder. If I'm lucky, you already understand that the odds of success are violently stacked against you. You are serious about building a startup and want practical, no-nonsense advice. A methodology that is real, human, honest, and not impossible to execute. One developed by an expert who has survived the trenches and has the scars to prove it. If you are looking for truth rather than feel-good platitudes or broad-stroke concepts, keep reading.

If, on the other hand, you bought this book hoping for a cheat code, a foolproof method to raise millions, or a step-by-step program to build a bulletproof business, I am not your guy. I'll give you your money back.

The framework I'm going to share with you is called Earn the Right (ETR) because impossibly hard work, not big ideas and wishful thinking, is what it takes to join the small number of founders who achieve success. A willingness to ask tough questions, think critically, listen to opposing opinions, make incredible sacrifices and hard decisions, then endure many,

many dark nights in pursuit of your big idea. In each chapter, you'll find ETR challenges meant to help move you along. On this journey, one of two things will happen: Either you'll embrace the framework and enjoy the process or you'll disagree so strongly that you'll gain clarity in your own approach. Either way, you win.

Whoever you are, however much you have in the bank, and no matter where you are on your founder's journey, if you're willing to step outside your own confirmation bias and do the work honestly, this book is built for you.

Before we go further, let's deal with some words you're probably already using. Every founder is racing to build a product. Every team calls itself innovative. Every startup claims to be disruptive. Every pitch deck believes itself to be funding ready.

Stop. Those aren't things you do. Those are outcomes. You don't get to say those words.

You don't do product. You don't do growth. You don't do innovation. You don't do funding. You don't do disruption. You don't get to name these attributes yourself. They are given to you. By the market. They are outcomes.

You don't build an Oscar-winning movie. You build a compelling story, assemble a talented team, craft each scene with precision, perfect the cinematography, refine the editing, and create something that resonates with audiences. The market then decides if they agree with you. First at the box office, then through critical acclaim, and maybe, just maybe, with an Oscar. But that's not up to you. That's an outcome.

Same with startups. You don't build a unicorn. You solve a real problem, assemble the right team, build effective systems, craft exceptional experiences, and create something that resonates with customers. The market decides if they agree with you. First with their wallets, then with their loyalty, and maybe, just maybe, with a billion-dollar valuation. But that's not up to you. That's an outcome.

What do you do? You do the work. Do the learning. Do the solving. Do the proof. You earn those titles. Visionaries do the work to earn the outcomes. Wannabes just declare them.

The market will tell you what you've built. Your job is to keep iterating until it tells you something you like.

I am full of passion for you and your idea and the process of helping you convert your big idea into an awesome reality. I am a great lover of ideas who thrives on working with awful founders attempting great things, great founders pursuing awful ideas, awful founders with awful ideas, and great founders on fire with great ideas. Which one are you? No matter. I am here in service to you. This book is your safe space to think and attempt and learn. This is a conversation between you and me; we can be deeply honest. As you work through this book, you have nothing to prove to me except your willingness to Earn the Right, going on your journey with me alongside you, like your own (virtual) fractional cofounder.

This journey is my raw, unfiltered, passionate manifesto on starting a startup. It's direct, no-nonsense, and with a never-ending sense of urgency that's more than a little intense and quite dense. I'm trying to pack a lot of experience, insight, informed opinions, and field-tested concepts into a tiny space, with the least amount of fluff possible, designed to get your attention and encourage you to figure out what's applicable to you.

The celebrated founder mentality of "fuck it, let's build a version 1 (an MVP, or minimum viable product), because if I build it, people will get it" is flawed. If you build it, no one is coming. Today's market has so few barriers to building stuff that simply introducing a great product is not quite enough to get you noticed (unless you have a mega network, and even then...). What I've seen work repeatedly is a different approach. Founders who say, "Before I build, I'm going to make sure it's *something people actually want*. My proof will be having a line of people ready to buy it. Buyers will be my source for validating assumptions, providing insights, and introducing new thoughts, before I go live." Convincing you to adopt that approach is basically the methodology behind this entire book.

Every founder starts at zero. No one starts with a product, customers, revenue, or a real clue how it will all play out. Everyone has a dream, a vision, and some level of arrogance that they can actually make this thing happen. Failure is the result of not doing everything in your power to turn your nothing into something. It's that simple.

Let's face it: In the startup world, not everyone has a foot on the same rung of the ladder. Some people are born ten rungs up, with access to networks, education, resources, and family that seem like magic to others. They can afford to live in San Francisco, attend Stanford, get their first investment from parents, or any other scenario that gives someone more shots. What they call luck, we call privilege.

If you're not starting from that place of privilege, accept it, understand it, complain about it, then embrace the fact that you will have to work harder. A lot harder. Be more creative, more resilient, more relentless, and most of all more patient, just to get to an equal place with someone with a stupid idea and family cash. It's not fair, but you have to play the game. So play it. That also means aggressively skilling up, because you have to overcompensate, so when luck does arrive, you are more than ready. But take heart: I'm not alone in believing that someone who comes from nothing and is able to manifest something is worth betting on.

If you are privileged, recognize it, but don't rely on it. Outside your circle, the market doesn't give a fuck about it. It only cares about the value you create. Privilege can get you investment, resources, even your first few customers, but it cannot get you market acceptance, longevity, leadership, or vision. You're still going to have to earn those.

For all first-time founders, this book is about encouraging and helping you to map your own journey. Every day, take one step forward so you can look back on the week and know you made progress. You are one tiny step away from failure. Walk away from the "gotta raise money" myth and just work it out. Your best access to money is in your capability to show you can capture some of the market, get paying customers, and delight the living shit out of them. Your challenge is to find the one narrow thing in the market space that you can do better than anyone else. Then build something great.

The way you become a billion-dollar company (a stupid goal to begin with) starts with your first sale, fighting tooth and nail for the first users and doing everything possible, maybe even improbable, to convert them to believers. Focus entirely on how you can thrill your customers. How you can deliver such incredible service to them that they become your fanatics. Your early, extreme customer-pleasing tactics might not scale, but that's part of the secret: doing unscalable things to build, to acquire, to retain, to delight, to support. Worry about processes later. Don't try to solve the entire market. Solve the narrowest slice and own that.

We know that most startups fail. The quicker you realize your startup is a massive experiment, the easier it is to prep yourself for the awful founder's journey ahead and understand what you need to focus on. I'm not here to tell you how to accelerate success, but I can tell you how to derail failure. That's the startup game in the early years. Success is survivability, simply staying alive. You're not trying to be "successful." You're walking backwards from failure, one shaky step at a time, hopefully in the direction of future success. So go out there and don't be one of the idiots that builds a nonsolution to a nonproblem no one was asking for in a nonexistent market.

Time is the one resource you can't get back. Every day you've spent dreaming about this startup instead of building it—gone. Every moment you've wasted waiting for the "right time" or the "perfect idea"—vanished. The clock is always ticking. You probably don't "got this." Not yet anyway. The odds are stacked against you, the competition is fierce, and the market doesn't give a fuck about your dreams.

But you're here now. Ready to stop thinking and start doing. Even on this journey to likely failure, you're probably still the right person to do it. Why? Because you've got something no one else has. You see a way, and you have the grit, the resilience, the fight, the delusion, and just the right amount of crazy to actually make it happen. It's this inexplicable blend of vision, passion, and sheer fucking audacity that made you crazy enough to think you could actually do it in the first place and that's what qualifies you to lead this ship. For now.

Be honest. Have you done everything possible up until this point to drive success? Probably not. Most of this book is about helping you take incremental steps forward until the practice of making 1 percent adjustments becomes a habit and earns you the right to keep going.

This is a marathon, not a sprint. Pace yourself, take care of yourself. This shit is grueling. And no one will understand what you are going through. But also run like there's a tiger chasing you, because there is. It's called irrelevance, obscurity, bankruptcy, death. And it's always hungry.

For many years, I have coached innovative people ranging from Y Combinator newbies to powerful teams within some of the world's largest companies. I've brought products to market and led innovation for global companies. And every now and again I founded my own startups. Over the course of my professional life, I have seen what leads to success and what nearly always ends in failure. The Earn the Right framework is the result, a process I have developed over time working with founders of all kinds. If you do the work, it works.

My goal is not to tell you how to win; there's no simple recipe. But I can tell you how to reduce the likelihood of failure, one step at a time. Earn the Right. Hurry slowly.

I want to give you a few words of actual encouragement. Everything changes, everything gets a touch easier, when it becomes crystal clear on a granular level how you will win customers. Actually win them. And spoiler alert, that happens when you focus on being the best at one specific thing for one specific audience.

You bought this book because you're ready to prove everyone wrong. This is your moment. Your shot at turning nothing into something. To transform your crazy ideas into reality. You want to know if you've got what it takes? There's only one way to find out. Start *earning the right* to change your fucking world.

PART ONE

MYTHS, MISINFORMATION, AND MOTIVATION

1
LET'S FUCKING GO

THESE ARE my opening words to you because I want you to go for your big idea. But first we need to blow up the myths and misinformation that cause too many first-time founders to never get started. It begins with the biggest hurdle, the one so many founders think is the first step, so many founders think is what defines them, and so many founders misunderstand the damaging impact of pursuing too early...

Money, Money, Money

You probably hoped this book would be a fine short story showing how you can effortlessly raise money and live your best founder's life. Pitch decks. Angel investors. Branded hoodies and the TechCrunch announcement that places you two levels higher than everyone else. It's what being a startup founder is, right, showing you have such a great idea that people are throwing millions at you?

There's a metric fuck-ton of advice being peddled out there and even more fundraising porn designed to make you believe the founder's absolute first step is to build a slick pitch deck and go beg for money. If you believe this myth, you will discover you are dead wrong, and your startup will be DOA (dead on arrival). If you're fundraising with no business results to show, if you aren't the domain expert (aka subject matter expert or SME), and if you don't already have a strong track record, you aren't getting any money (nor should you). Period. Even worse, you are going to spend what precious little money you have trying to raise money. Money you could have spent or invested actually moving your business forward, one inch at a time.

There is very little that compensates for traction—specifically, revenue traction—when trying to raise money. If your business, product, service, idea is so innovative, so amazing, so fantastic, so impactful, where is the line out the door eager to buy? Think about money like this: Money is jet fuel to existing momentum. If you are doing nothing, then money on top of nothing is still nothing. When you are doing something, then money on top of something leads to something bigger. So if you have nothing to show, no traction, no clock speed, no one is going to give you money with the possible exception of the three Fs: friends, family, and fools.

A quick question: Why do you think you need to raise money? I know you're thinking, "To hire engineers to build my product, dummy!" or "To pay for AdWords because that's my entire marketing strategy!" Right now, with the commoditization of coding and the accessibility of talent, if you can't figure out how to move your startup forward without a big cash infusion, you're not cut out for this game. The amount of time founders waste paying for email lists, automation tools, and other "growth hacks" when they could be actually building something of value is staggering. You'll wake up three months from now, your startup in the exact same spot, with nothing to show but a string of rejections, less money than you started with, and three months lost against your targeted launch date.

Before we dive in, some bad news: The best product doesn't win. The best team doesn't win. The fastest to learn, iterate, and rerelease wins. That's what we call "clock speed." The winners are the ones who can escape their own confirmation bias, see through the romance of their idea, and recognize reality faster than anyone else. They're the ones who can pivot on a dime when the market tells them they're wrong.

From the start, you need to make something *meaningful and measurable* happen.

Investors want to see that you can create something out of nothing. They want to see that when all the odds are stacked against you, through some magic of grit, smarts, and luck, you manage to literally make something happen. They are investing first in YOU, the founder. Also the idea, and potentially a big market, and the leadership team, but mainly in you. To get their cash, you have to demonstrate your capability to make magic happen while intelligently pivoting along the way. Let me reemphasize that last bit: The fastest founder to learn, iterate, and rerelease wins. Not the best team. Not the best product. The fastest founder who can pivot accordingly.

I understand you're not going to believe me. You've made your mind up. You are convinced you have to raise money. So fine (begrudgingly), let's get real about fundraising.

Every investor has their own rubric, their own unique set of questions they think matter. Think of them as distinct from each other as snowflakes. And despite the mountain of cash they sit on, the resources that make you think they are the word of god, most investors have never owned, operated, or even worked at a startup. They don't actually know what it takes. Most have opinions, and some of them might even be grounded in truth, but most investors actually add negative value to a startup with bad advice. Don't be seduced into thinking they know more than you do about your idea.

That said, most investors look for four core things. We'll go deeper into this later, but here's the short list:

1. An attractive market: How tough is the competition?
2. Market-leading product potential: How different are you?
3. A founder and team that can pull it off: How strong is your team?
4. A fund "returner": How much money do they need to make on this investment? (Duh.)

They'll also be weighing if they want to be married to you for the next seven years, because that's how long this relationship is likely to last. You'll want to think about this too, because it's easier to get a divorce than to get an investor off your cap table. All great startups are born from solving a big problem for many potential customers better than their incumbents can and creating a significantly superior product that is hard to copy. That too is what investors care about.

So since you are determined to pursue money, here are your funding options.

Bootstrapping: This is where you MUST start. Roll up your sleeves and get your hands dirty. Use every resource at your disposal: your time, your skills, your network. It's hard work and it's your ticket to freedom. Every step you take on your own dime is a step towards higher valuation and proof that you might just be able to do this thing. Prove you can hustle for results. That's the kind of founder investors want to back.

Angel investors: The real builders of progress of the startup world. High-net-worth individuals who choose to bet on you before you're anything. Gambling their own money, choosing to take a chance on an unproven founder with a big vision. Be prepared: They know exactly what they are looking for.

Incubators and accelerators: Boot camp for startups. These are programs by the industry or sector that might give you some cash, a ton of mentorship, and a network of other founders. Normally, you are giving up a slice of equity, so beware of predatory ones that make you pay to play. For a first-time founder with their shit together, this could be a hugely attractive way to learn and accomplish what these organizations claim to do: speed up your journey.

That's it. Those are your options. I intentionally did not list venture capital (VC) in this list, because it's not worthy of a mention until you have traction. Money is earned, not given, and the best way to show you have earned it is to *convince a customer* to pay for it.

In case I wasn't 100 percent clear, you don't need outside funding to begin to build your business. Chasing funding too early in your life cycle is more of a death sentence. It distracts, discourages, dilutes your ownership, and adds unproductive pressure to your life.

Ask yourself, "If I'm not able to raise money, is that the end of my journey?" Fuck no. So forget your damn pitch deck for a minute. Give me ten things you *could* do right now that would make your startup better, clearer, stronger, such as perhaps the following:

- Dedicate some time to improving your clock speed.
- Get into "traffic" to learn from the market. (I'm not talking about the morning commute. I'm talking about getting your idea, your product, your solution in front of real people. It's about creating a perpetual feedback loop, where you're constantly learning from your market. Get out there, in it, talking, colliding with reality.)
- Work to find a truly better way, not just an incremental change or solution tweak.

By the end of the week, can you write an email to yourself describing everything you accomplished for your startup this week, big and small? Do this every week. Make it a habit. Get to work. Your imaginary investors can wait.

Failure and Luck Are a Package Deal

You're going to fail. Over and over again. Get used to it, embrace it, learn from it. Someone once said this to me and I love it: "Failure is the tuition you pay for a real education in startups." The key is to fail fast, fail cheap, and fail forward.

Failing doesn't mean you won't launch a product or find some customers. But ultimately it means the market speaks and you haven't created a sustainable business. It's a phenomenal way to start your founder journey, knowing failure is almost inevitable. In fact, the chance of failure rounded to the nearest whole number is probably 100 percent. That's not me being a dick, it's just stats.

Why do startups fail? Is it because the founders are stupid? Perhaps. More often it's because they get trapped in their own echo chamber, their own confirmation bias, their own arrogance. They fail to ask themselves or the market the hard questions and actually listen and respond to the answers. Actively listening and responding could save them from a long, awful journey to extinction. Startups are experiments, and experiments by design include failure. If we knew all the answers, it wouldn't be an experiment, and every startup would succeed. The real danger is not in the experiment. Trying is necessary. The danger is in not hearing the feedback, or even worse, ignoring it. The elusive goal for your experiments is discovering the sweet spot between cost, speed, and value: getting to market fast with a product that delights customers and generates actual revenue.

You're never going to be able to eliminate all risk, but you can mitigate it. No one can guarantee success, but you can increase your odds incrementally. I propose a continual series of 1 percent adjustments that reduce the likelihood of failure. Think of this effort as earning your right to win, one hard-fought battle at a time.

The winners learn the quickest, escape their own confirmation bias, see through the romance of their idea, and recognize reality. Almost every monster success did a dramatic pivot based on listening to the market signals and iterating like their life depended on it, starting out with one business idea, then seeing real opportunity beckoning from a different direction.

The biggest names in tech almost all have a pivot moment. Slack started as a game company. Pinterest began as a mobile shopping app. Instagram was originally a location-based check-in app. Shopify? They were trying to sell snowboards. None of these companies succeeded because of their original ideas. They succeeded because they had the capability to recognize when their initial concept wasn't working or was too limiting. They were willing to summon up the speed (and guts?) to pivot *into* something that the market was maybe hinting it wanted more. That's the power of clock speed in action.

One in three startups pivot before landing on what enables them to scale. That's what makes this whole startup thing an experiment.

Along the way you will hear hundreds of nos and 90 percent of the rejections you get won't even give you the real reason. You'll hear a lot of "not my space" or "not sure we can add value." In reality, they just don't want to offend you. Every founder has endured every possible form of rejection on their journey. It's part of the rite of passage. The secret is that with each try you get better, your understanding of the problem deepens, your solution iterates, you begin to speak to the concerns of your potential users (and funders).

I know you want a massive market, but a massive market starts with knowing it's a massive market, then building a *small network within that massive market*. Once you show you can win in the smallest niche, it becomes easier to shift to the next-sized one, to expand out, to build out, to grow. Small wins are the foundation—traction and revenue.

Ignore the TikTok of hypergrowth. Think lean. Minimize the number of steps in everything you do, everything you build, everything you process. Simplify to lower the points of failure. Fewer points mean less chance of failure.

Most of all, act as if you are not fighting to create the next unicorn. In reality, this is not what most people are building. While many first-time founders dream about the billions they'll make, practically speaking, you should be fighting hard to get to highly achievable exit numbers. Bootstrap your company. Get to $2 million in revenue and sell for $20 million. That sounds fantastic, but it's genuinely achievable, not some ridiculously inflated goal. And it's far less ridiculous than bragging to a VC that "very soon" you're going to get to $100 million in revenue.

Take a closer look before you dismiss the idea of aiming lower. Getting to $2 million in revenue works out to be $160,000 a month, or 500 people paying $300 a month. Can you find 500 people in the whole world that might pay you $300 a month for your service, or 1,000 customers at $150, and so on? If your idea is so fab, surely you can find those few people out of the billions of buyers on the planet. Sell to people who can afford your solution, the customers who pay for convenience because they value their time. They are the ones far more likely to recognize and pay for the value. As you run this gauntlet, build a real brand, not just a mirage, because that's where lasting value lies.

So with that, let's talk about luck.

Increase Your Luck

Luck is not about waiting for lightning to strike. It's about building a long lightning rod and running around in a thunderstorm wearing a metal jacket. You have to create your own luck.

Founders think success is the idea, the raising money, hiring rock stars—and it is—but time and again there are these small signals that separate the incredible founders. They consistently have the capability to recognize and capitalize on luck when it shows up. Because luck in some form is always showing up. The difference is in the people who hear it, see it, and seize it.

Too many founders are so focused on their grand vision that they miss the small opportunities right in front of them. Waiting for the big break instead of creating a thousand tiny breaks that compound.

Luck isn't something that happens to you. What others call luck, you should call hard work, time spent earning it. Every person you meet, every article you read, every conference you attend, every skill you develop, every experiment you run—these are all potential vectors for luck because you are increasing your surface area for luck. What looks like serendipity is actually predictable, because serendipity favors only the prepared.

To be clear, successful founders often hugely downplay the role of luck in their journey. They want us to believe they did it all. But if you look closely, you'll see the one thing or the one moment that changed everything.

Timing is luck. Market shifts are luck. But the reality is you create luck by fighting. Luck is nurturing that one customer who becomes your evangelist. It's the random stumbling into an engineer who turns your half-baked idea into a thing. It's meeting that cofounder who complements your skills perfectly. It's discovering that one killer feature that makes your product irresistible. And most importantly, it's being ready to recognize and seize these opportunities when they appear.

So how do you prepare your mind? How do you increase your surface area for luck?

Be in motion. Be in the arena. Constantly. The more you do, the more opportunities you create. Send that cold email. Attend that meetup. Do that thing. Learn that thing. Run that crazy experiment. You cannot win the lottery without buying a ticket.

Be aware. Pay attention. Listen. Observe. Connect the dots that others miss. The world is constantly giving you feedback—half the battle is shutting up long enough to hear it.

Be flexible. Success is a drunken walk of constant course correction based on the feedback you're getting. The capability to *intelligently* pivot, take detours, backtrack, blow it all up. Your job isn't to stick to a plan. It's to figure out what the fuck is actually working and double down on that.

Be persistent. Luck isn't a one-time event. It's a numbers game. The more at bats you have, the more chances you have to hit a home run. It's that simple. Ignore the failures, the ghosting, the shitty feedback—it's all just data. You need only one to reply, one to say yes, one to engage.

Be ready. None of this matters if you are not prepared to open the door when opportunity knocks. That means doing the work. Building the skills. Creating the network. Laying the groundwork. So you don't find luck and piss it away.

Luck has a dark side because bad luck exists. Sometimes the market shifts, your customer's budget disappears, your advocate is fired, your engineer has a medical emergency. Sometimes a global pandemic shuts down the entire fucking world. Resilience isn't about avoiding bad luck. It's about being able to take a punch and keep moving forward. It's about having the grit to turn setbacks into comebacks. It's about being antifragile—getting stronger in the face of adversity instead of breaking.

Timing is one of the few items you cannot control. Not really. You can try to increase your odds by being hyperaware of the market or consumer behavior. You can build in public to get real-time feedback. The finality of all of this is that timing is everything. And timing is just another word for luck. Being too early is the same as being wrong. Being too late means fighting for scraps in a crowded market. But being just right? You got lucky! I've seen so many founders get lucky once and think they're a genius. They start believing their own hype because they have the zeros in the bank account to prove it. They stop doing the things, the hustle, the fight that made them lucky in the first place. And they crash and burn.

Build the Luck Muscle

The best founders I know have this almost supernatural ability to turn bad luck into good luck. They see the opportunity in every crisis. They believe the expression that "a crisis is a terrible thing to waste." They use new constraints as a driving catalyst for creativity. They turn obstacles into advantages. True founders see a different future, where startup success is not about doing what a bigger company does but cheaper or better—it's about fundamentally changing the way something is done.

The real mindfuck: The more you practice creating luck, the luckier you'll get. It's a skill. Like any skill, it improves with practice. So... start practicing. Remember, luck is not evenly distributed, but it is more evenly distributed than you think. It's not about having one big lucky break. Luck is asymmetric: lots of small lucky breaks compound over time into big wins.

And finally, luck favors the bold. Not the reckless, but the bold. The ones willing to take calculated risks. The ones willing to put themselves out there. The ones willing to fail publicly and get back up. Once you've accepted the absolute near certainty of failure and the role you can play in creating luck, this next mindset helps to frame your journey.

"Everything is your fault." It's such a foul phrase, but it is the best way to ground everything in truth. After all, as a founder, you are the company. Can't raise money? Your fault. You pitched wrong, to the wrong people, with the wrong words, wrong product, wrong something. Didn't get that cofounder to join your journey? That's your fault too. You failed to adequately convey the vision, show the potential, or create something they wanted to be part of. Customer churn too high? Your product isn't solving their problem well enough. Team not performing? You hired wrong or you're not leading effectively. When every crappy thing that falls apart is your fault, what do you do?

Become Your Best CEO

Another hard truth. Every founder starts out as a shitty CEO.

Since we've already established that everything is your fault, let's consider for a moment your qualifications to be a CEO. You, the best CEO? Who are we kidding! Literally everyone knows you have no idea what you're doing. You have no leadership experience, no sales skills, no product expertise, no financial acumen, and probably no engineering skills. You're basically jumping off a cliff and trying to assemble a parachute on the way down. Join the club. But you do have one thing that really, really matters: the founder magic, the vision.

It's why even though you have no sales experience, there's no better salesperson than you, and not because you are

Literally everyone knows you have no idea what you're doing... But you do have one thing that really, really matters: **the founder magic, the vision.**

naturally great at sales. Passionate founders figure out how to be what's called a "middler"—they learn through practice exactly how to talk to prospects, how to hack the product to show what the prospect wants, how to have an informed, honest conversation about their competition. They deeply know the feature gaps, the future of the product and of the industry. Motivated by their beliefs, they become true evangelists with a compelling conviction that no sales team can surpass.

Right now everyone knows you and your product are lacking, everyone knows you're lying (or at least exaggerating) about what your business can do. Surprisingly, happily for you, we don't care. No one is buying the "today" version. They're buying into the future, a future we believe no one will be better able to sell than you.

The bargain I propose is that if we accept your absolute awfulness as a CEO, in return you will commit to being the heart and soul of this startup. Your first year as a founder is a trial by fire. It's a year of reckoning and hard truths, but also the year that molds you into the leader your company needs. After that first year, all the inexperience that your investors, employees, and customers tolerated is no longer acceptable. It's time to level up. The clock is running. Are you a better CEO today than yesterday? You can be if you dedicate yourself to knowing the problem you're solving better than anyone. To understand your customers' pain points on a visceral level. Everyone around you is trusting you to have the vision for where this business needs to go, even if you can't always articulate it clearly. We are betting on you to never lose this "Holy shit, we might actually pull this off" vibe that can inspire a team, woo investors, and win over customers.

Think about Steve Jobs. The guy was kicked out of his own company and labeled a lunatic. Yet when Apple needed saving, they brought back that very same lunatic. And he saved them. Why? Because he was *their* lunatic. He had the vision and the audacity an outside CEO could never replicate.

The inevitable failures you face are not your enemy. Complacency is. Arrogance is. Ignorance is. Embracing the "everything is your fault" mindset isn't about beating yourself up. It's about taking full ownership of your journey. It's about recognizing that you have the power to influence every aspect of your startup, and with that power comes the responsibility to learn, adapt, and keep pushing forward, no matter what obstacles you face. Here are just some of the ways to embrace the suck and become the CEO you need to be.

Build a culture of experimentation and rapid learning from day one. Foster an environment where it's okay to try things, fuck up fast, and learn faster. Where everyone is expected to think and act like an owner. Because that's what it takes.

Obey the law of yes or no. If it's not a yes (from a customer, an investor, a team member), then it's a no. There are no maybes. Don't settle, don't compromise, don't waste your time and energy on anything less than spectacular, the things that move the needle. You don't get that time back. And especially in the startup stage, progress over time is how you are measured. (Clock speed again.)

The only metrics that matter are your time to market, time to revenue, time to feedback, time to learning, time to battle testing. And anything that gets in the way of these core metrics is not worth tracking. Know your metrics, instrument everything, and measure what matters. Don't get caught up in vanity metrics. Identify numbers that tell you if you're creating real value. Numbers are the North Star that convert your gut to fact and turn feedback into insights.

Starting now, commit to developing a relentless focus. Stop fucking around on everything else, wasting time and resources. This insane, almost psychotic devotion to do what has to be done to get to the next step—what I call "earning the right"—is the necessary level of concentration.

Recognize that your journey is a series of oxymorons. You have only one job, but you're also wearing many hats. You must have laser focus, but you can't lose sight of the big picture. You must have psychotic delusions about your capabilities to execute but make sure you don't act as if you're infallible. A specialist and a generalist, a strategist and an operator, confident and humble. This insane capability to go from worker in the trenches to drone overhead, alternating with ease and at the right cadence. It's an impossible demand: Be focused but also be wide, think big but also be extremely narrow, isolate your impact but make sure it's not too isolated. Being able to balance all that is exactly what makes you the right person for the job.

Grit Makes Great

The great founders, the ones who change the game and leave a dent in the universe, they have this almost superhuman ability to context switch like it's a fucking art form. They're down in the trenches, getting their hands dirty, sweating the details, and grinding out the work. But then, in the blink of an eye, they're in the sky, thinking big, surveying the landscape, seeing the patterns and connections that others miss. None of this is easy. None of it just happens. You have to choose to work at it every damn day.

The truly great founders don't stay "failed." Not because they never face setbacks or challenges but because they refuse to quit. They stay focused, create extraordinary products, team up with remarkable cofounders, assemble a band of loyal pirates who bleed for the shared vision, and they persist through countless near-death experiences.

Grit is and will always be the biggest superpower you have. Along your founder's journey, you will meet a load of different investor types, but the angels who have been at it for more than a hot minute know one thing clearly: When you find a founder who has the spark and the grit, write the check and say thank you. It will all work out fine. Grit is grit is grit, but we can break it down further.

Decisional grit: Making the tough calls when the right choice and the easy one diverge. It's having the balls to bet it all on red when everyone else is screaming at you to walk away from the roulette table.

Endurance grit: This isn't just about "toughing it out." It's about adapting, learning, and getting stronger through challenges. It's what keeps you going after you've made those tough decisions and the shit has hit the fan.

You're going to need both types of grit in spades. Running a startup isn't a sprint or even a marathon. It's more like an ultramarathon through a minefield, uphill, in the pouring rain, wearing cheap flip-flops. Grit is the number one trait above everything else that is on every single VC team rubric. But—and this is crucial—endurance without judgment is a pitfall. Don't be the founder who spends years trying to resuscitate an idea that's long lost its pulse. The truly great founders recognize when to pivot and when to persevere. Having that discernment and courage is what separates great from good.

And for fuck's sake, be a solo founder, sure, but don't try to do every single thing on your own. And don't hire muppets. If you have to explain yourself constantly, change people.

If you have to manage the team every day, change people. You don't have the margin for substandard work. Surround yourself with mentors, advisors, investors who have been there and done it. Not the wannabe gurus or self-appointed thought leaders, but real-deal founders who have the scars, the exits, the war stories to prove it. Listen to their hard-earned wisdom but never outsource your thinking. Success doesn't come from following every bit of advice. It comes from being smart enough to differentiate the advice, check the credibility of the source, and decide what aligns with your vision, goals, and style. As someone once said, you wouldn't ask a nun for sex advice.

Be honest about your contributions. Make sure you're the right person for the job. Learn, listen, be humble, be determined. These are the founders who win, the ones with the grit and resilience to find a way when the shit, as it surely will, hits the fan. No one needs you to be a great leader today. We need you to be able to prove that what you are building has value. Have a commitment to excellence that those around you would think outlandish.

Through it all, never, ever confuse effort with results. No one gives a shit how hard you work or how passionate you are. The market is a ruthless arbiter of value. So create real value or perish. All of this is to say that startups are more of a science than a wish list. You have to go where the research and the results take you. Start with your core vision, but don't get permanently attached to it. You're probably more wrong than right. Let your eyes be open enough to see something better or iterative when it comes your way, and to a certain degree follow the path.

The founder's journey isn't about money, failure, luck, or being a great CEO from day one. It's about commitment to the vision, a desire to make a dent in the universe. It's about showing up, day after day, ready to face whatever challenges come your way. It's about being the fastest learner, the quickest thinker, with an insane focus, and a mastery in leading a tribe. Success often appears overnight, but it's almost always a decade in the making. Amazon took seven years to turn a profit. Airbnb didn't gain traction until three years after launch. Tesla took seventeen years to report its first full profitable year.

In the end, your founder's story is about having the courage to step into the arena, to risk failure, and to suffer real heartbreak. To build something that matters, something you're insanely proud of, whether or not you get the glory (or the cash). *Something that people actually want.* The world depends on crazy fools like you who think they can change things. Who are stubborn and delusional enough to try. And who might just pull it off. Stay humble, stay hungry, stay foolish.

So, as you step into the arena, remember this: You're not just working, you're creating a legacy. You're not looking for luck, you're forging resilience. You're cultivating grit and determination that will serve you for the rest of your life, regardless of the outcome of this particular venture.

Your Personal Metrics

The founder's journey is going to demand more of you than anything you've ever done before. It's the ultimate uncharted territory. You're going to hear the words "impostor syndrome" a lot. It's easy to get lost, frustrated, and feel like a fake or a failure. Having some ways to check in on yourself can help you course correct and keep you sane. Ask yourself truthfully, "Am I doing any of this important shit or just acting busy?"

Embrace the suck. Own your role. Be the CEO your startup needs, even when—especially when—you feel like you have no idea what you're doing. Because in the end, that's what separates the winners from the losers in this game. Not the brilliance of their idea or the size of their war chest, but their ability to earn it, day in and day out, in the face of relentless uncertainty and unforgiving odds.

Leave no stone unturned. Evaluate everything, have an eye on prioritization, impact, and opportunity, but be wise enough to give every possibility a moment of thought.

Build a diverse network. It's a fact: The more diverse your ecosystem in terms of race, gender, industry, skills, perspectives, whatever, the more potential vectors for luck you have.

Experiment. Run cheap, fast tests constantly. Create feedback loops that allow you to quickly identify what's working and what isn't. The faster you can iterate, the more chances you have to get lucky.

Stay curious. Read, not just in your industry but across disciplines. Some of the best innovations come from applying ideas from one field to another. You just never know where your next big breakthrough will come from.

Build in the public view. Share your journey. Document your learnings. Engage with your audience. The more you put yourself out there, the more chances you create for serendipity.

Be value driven. Help others without expectation of return. Share your knowledge. Offer your skills. The more value you put into the world, the more the world tends to give back.

Cultivate a bias towards action. Don't wait for perfect information. Don't wait for permission. Just do something. Anything. Movement creates opportunity.

Hopefully this mayhem of ideas might have earned me the right to introduce you to a framework designed to guide first-time founders. My aim is to help you mitigate risk and, in the process, avoid some major missteps. I never tell my clients what to do. I ask hard questions and offer informed opinions. It's your decision to choose what's right for you. Judgment cannot be outsourced. You've got to own it for yourself.

But first, you have to start. You have to commit. You have to say those beautiful, terrifying words: Let's fucking go.

2
GET READY FOR AI

THERE'S NO point in trying to ignore artificial intelligence (AI). It's here, it's massive, it's magical, it's incredible. It's the most powerful accelerator we've ever seen in the startup world. AI allows you to run at warp speed, deliver content, provide insights, expand your thoughts, operate faster. Incredible. Period. And it's going to get fundamentally better at doing literally everything.

But it's also incredible for everyone else who uses it too. It's giving everyone who masters it the same superpowers.

Think of AI as an accelerator like money. It makes an idiot a 10x idiot, and it makes a visionary a 10x visionary. It can't craft something out of nothing because it needs the raw input, the data, the problem to solve, the understanding of the market. If you're building garbage, AI will help you build garbage faster. If you don't deeply understand your market, your problem, or your customer, AI is going to accelerate your failure, not prevent it. Every shortcut you think you've found with AI? Your competitors have found it too.

The amazing thing about AI is that it actually creates more work for you faster. It cuts the bullshit work, so more of your minutes are spent on the high-value, high-impact work that requires analysis, strategizing, and decision-making—the work that demands critical thinking.

Sure, you can ask AI for ten business ideas and run that playbook, but if you're reading this book that's not your approach.

AI has to be a foundational pillar of anything you're building, not a bolt-on or afterthought, no matter what you do or what service you provide. But AI isn't a substitute for you doing the real work of being a founder.

There's a tension between opportunity and obligation. There are clearly opportunities in what AI offers: its immense potential to provide insights at an unparalleled scale and to accelerate innovation and efficiency. But there are also obligations: the responsibility that comes with having access to such power and the need to know your market deeply, truly understand the problem you are solving at its micro level, and always ask the right questions.

AI Changes Everything (and Nothing)

The fundamentals of building a successful startup haven't changed. In fact, they've become more important than ever because when everyone has the same superpowers, the difference between success and failure comes down to execution—how well you use all available resources.

In a world where anyone can generate a landing page in seconds, build a high-impact hook for a Facebook ad, generate financial models, integrate opportunities, AND build prototypes without coding, what separates the winners from the pack? The same thing that always has. A deep understanding of the problem you're solving and the ability to execute based on that understanding. Or more simply: Build a product people actually want and will pay for. If your strategy is wrong, if your product is off the mark, AI will help you, but it's your foundational knowledge that will tell you why.

The irony of AI is that it makes human judgment more valuable, not less. Critical thinking is your superpower, learning to asking better questions. AI gives great answers but only to the questions you are smart enough to ask. Even with AI assistance, you still have to be the one to see the patterns, the signs, the nuance. The signals that make you think you have found a space that you can enter and win. You're still the one who has to make the strategic decisions and determine where real value lies. No one can do that for you.

The New Gold Rush

Don't go out and buy every AI tool, but don't just settle for popular default options either. You should explore and play with everything, break things, see what sticks, see the use cases, the application of AI, the business models, the everything. This is the new gold rush, and fools will rush in. You have to work out where you sit because there is opportunity in the gold but also in everything surrounding it. You can't afford to sit on the sidelines pretending you don't really understand AI.

Remember who really got rich in the gold rush: not just the ones who struck gold, but the ones who sold the picks, shovels, and supplies. They built businesses serving the rush itself. Today's AI picks and shovels? They're the tools, platforms, and infrastructure that power all these AI experiments. Sometimes the real opportunity isn't in striking gold, but in enabling the search.

Ninety-eight percent of AI startups right now are like the flashlight app on your iPhone. You might not remember this scenario, but it was brilliant, turning your $600 phone into a $1 flashlight, it was pure innovation. Everyone paid that ninety-nine cents. Everyone used it. Until it didn't matter anymore. It became a basic feature, then an unnecessary app, then completely irrelevant, table stakes: My Garmin watch has a flashlight feature. But we need those flashlight apps; those early creators, those maniacs, those lunatics; those somewhat stupid ideas to push the market forward and shake out what actually matters. The market often needs pointless, countless failures before we understand what we can do, and need.

So explore the ridiculous, just don't mistake novelty for lasting value. Build the flashlight app of AI if that is the entry point, but your job is to try and understand what comes next. Always remember people thought sending 140-character messages or paying to rent someone's bedroom was stupid.

Most of the AI ads in your feed are pointless, but hidden in that chaos are the initial seeds of what will work. The same goes for AI-powered everything—design tools, coding assistants, marketing platforms. Most are garbage, but the 2 percent that aren't are the ones that likely understood at a foundational level the problem they wanted to solve.

We're in the phase of AI madness and exploration, and that's where innovation happens. So go ahead, do what you have to do to learn. The beauty of this moment is that very few people really get AI. Most of the market is learning on the fly. The quickest team to learn wins. But hear me when I say that the founders who are succeeding today are those who get their hands dirty.

You can't outsource what a founder has to know and do to succeed. You have to be fully in it. You need to be in the trenches.

AI, Part 2 Comes at the End

This chapter is divided into two parts for a reason. What you've just read is about acknowledging the potential power of AI as an accelerator and force multiplier. This chapter happens early so I can stress that *before you dive into how to use AI, you need to master the why.*

Now more than ever you must understand your market and your position before you jump in. If you don't deeply know your customer's pain and your market's dynamics, no amount of AI will help you win. Your job now is not to become an AI expert first. It's to become an expert in your market, your customer, and your problem. Only then can you Earn the Right to use AI effectively.

Get back to the basics. Don't cheat. AI will be waiting for you when you've done the work of learning what it takes to be a (very human) founder.

Get Ready to Earn the Right

Up to this point we've been working around the edges of what it means to be a founder. These early days are a shitshow filled with unknowns, insecurities, and the dark scary

You can't afford to sit on the sidelines **pretending you don't really understand AI.**

shadow of total failure. What will get you through is asking questions, lots of them. Pushing to get real answers. Listening deeply. Without wishful thinking or bias confirmation. It's 100 percent true that hope is not a strategy. And if you build it, mostly they will not come.

This sounds grim, but I am here to encourage and support you. To give you the confidence to ignore the phony how-to advice of three steps or thirty days that guarantee brilliant success. Hurry slowly. Spend as little money as possible. Dedicate yourself to doing something *every day* that chips away at the 0 percent chance of success every new idea faces. Time to get serious because this is how you Earn It.

There's a dangerous mythology in startup culture: these perfectly crafted bullshit stories of visionary founders who supposedly knew *exactly* what to do at every step.

Every single founder, even the ones you and I both view as titans of industry, had the terrifying moment of crossing from "I have this vision" to "Holy shit, I'm actually doing this." That first step is terrifying. The hero stories leave out the sleepless nights, the constant self-doubt, the waves of anxiety, the fact you are probably delusional and making a massive mistake.

The hero stories leave out the most important truth—the unknown is just that: unknown. No amount of preparation, research, or planning can eliminate it. Once you accept that uncertainty is fundamental to the journey, once you understand that stepping into that unknown is precisely what makes you an entrepreneur, you'll stop measuring yourself against these sanitized startup deities. Their stories are written in retrospect, edited for maximum inspiration, stripped of all the doubt and chaos and confusion. Your story is being written right now...

The real superpower isn't having all the answers—it's being willing to move forward without them. To build in the dark. To start climbing when you can't see the whole staircase. That's what separates founders. Not fearlessness but the courage to act despite the fear.

So when you're questioning everything, when your confidence wavers, remember: You're not alone. You're not less capable because you're scared. You're a founder because you keep moving forward despite the fear. The hero stories come later, written in hindsight, written by the winners. Right now, you're exactly where you need to be. Welcome to the real founder's journey.

In the following chapters, you'll work through a proven framework. It's a logical sequence of problems, challenges, mysteries, hard choices, painful truths—all the real stuff a founder faces. Working through this slow build teaches you a process for how to think about and evaluate your business. Stay with me here. Focus on the outcome: *risk mitigation*. At each stage, you are incrementally reducing your likelihood of failure or, put another way, increasing your chances of success. There's no cheat code buried in these pages. No one can give you the foolproof formula to rocket your business to monster scale. But you can Earn the Right to build a viable business if *you* do the work.

Emphasis on "you" because AI has arrived and it's a game-changer. The penultimate chapter goes deeper into a discussion of AI, but here are some things you need to know now. Code is no longer the big, expensive mystery it once was. While previously the bottleneck was accessing technical expertise, now it's reaching distribution channels, aka users. Learning to use AI, and you must, doesn't alter the fact that your enduring competitive edge rests in your deep understanding of the market and your ability to capitalize on that knowledge. AI won't build your startup for you. It's not the new cheat code. But skillfully deployed, it can significantly amplify your efforts, allowing you to compete in ways that were totally unimaginable just a few years ago. You still need to do the insanely hard work of becoming a founder.

For literally every startup founder, the first iteration of everything you do is 80 to 90 percent pure junk. Accept it. The value is in the 10 to 20 percent you've discovered through experimentation, exploration, and revision. Why does this matter? Because the days of loose VC money sloshing around and without much due diligence being showered on untested founders, being apportioned out to "visionary" projects and random self-proclaimed "disrupters" is over. As Airbnb CEO Brian Chesky famously said in 2022, "It's like we're all in a nightclub and the lights just came on."

This isn't an opinion. It's a fact. I know from personal experience what it takes in this much more sober market to make you eligible for investment, to earn the infusion of capital that makes it possible to bring your business to the next stage.

PART TWO

THE EARN THE RIGHT FRAMEWORK

3

EARN THE RIGHT
TO SOLVE A PROBLEM, PART 1

ASPIRING FOUNDERS sort themselves into two groups: the ones who want to do only the fun work of talking about their idea and playing at being a disruptor and the ones who grit their teeth and do the awful, boring work required to go beyond easy assumptions and keep iterating. Any investor can see the difference between the ones who understand that everything is on the line here and those who don't. Between the ones who think they know everything and the ones who are relentlessly questioning and problem-solving. The ones who understand the crucial importance of building their business on the best possible, strongest, and most market-tested foundation.

This Is Where Founders Flounder

Successful founders' methodology includes freethinking. Being able to recognize that your current obsession is irrelevant. Moving on to prioritize the things that need fixing now. Expanding your mindset beyond the binary. Too many founders see a two-track approach between build and commercialization. They say, "I know what I want to build, but I just need to get some customers. I need to hire some people to get me customers." No, you don't.

Keep bootstrapping and DIY-ing until you've got something that someone gives a fuck about. Train yourself to stop compartmentalizing the elements of your business. Learn to see how they are all connected and can be worked on simultaneously. This is the value to time to work ratio. Spending your limited resources strategically to yield the greatest return.

As a first-time founder, you have one game and it's how you execute. That's it. Keep making the moves that bring you one inch closer to having a real solution to a real problem. So let's begin with the problem. I'm with you.

Honor Your Catalyst Objective

Too easily founders get drawn into resolving the latest daily crisis. Maybe you're buried in busywork. Or maybe, after a burst of inspiration, you're stagnating. It happens to everyone. But exceptional founders aren't firefighters; they're architects. They're building, not reacting.

Can you name the one thing that will move the needle more than anything else you can do? That's your *catalyst objective*. Use the Pareto principle to find the 20 percent of focus areas that will yield 80 percent of the results. Evaluate potential gain. Eliminate smaller concerns. Then execute relentlessly.

Goals and objectives are not interchangeable. A goal is your ultimate target, like hitting $1 million in annual recurring revenue by year-end. Objectives are the functional requirements to achieve it.

Honoring your catalyst objective is damn hard. This is not a cute mantra. Treat this one-hour rule of peak performance as a binding contract, not a suggestion. No context switching allowed. Interruptions are the enemy; focus is the ally. Don't succumb to "urgent" emails, quick calls, or Slack notifications. When you're in your war room, make every second count.

Once you identify your catalyst objective and commit to working towards it *every day*, you've got a path forward. Skip it and you're the problem holding you back. This is how you exit firefighting mode. This is how you start to lead to get real results.

The Solution is Not Step One

Founder, you only have one job, amid the chaos of the other "one jobs" demanding your attention.

The only job that matters, right now: Build a product people want.

The keywords here are not "build" or "product" but rather "people want." Before you write a line of code, go off trying to raise money, hire a cofounder, quit your job, before you literally do anything else, you must be 100 percent certain you have found a problem that is legitimately, verifiably, urgently in need of a solution.

Sound simple? It's close to impossible.

This chapter is not about your solution. Forget your solution exists. It's irrelevant right now. If you mention your solution or your startup in this chapter, then you missed the point. If you answer any question with "I" or "we," pull yourself out of your constricting solution bubble for a second. This chapter challenges you to look objectively at the problem. Just for a hot second.

We're going back to the beginning, the reason your startup has the right to exist. It has to start with the problem you are solving. Your so-called solution isn't even a character in this story yet. Most founders do this backwards. They assume they know the problem, fall in love with their solution, then race to solution delivery. The reality is right now your solution doesn't matter.

Okay, there are exceptions. If you're already an expert in the field, if you have the data in your head, and if you're just sure upon sure, then go for it. Sometimes finding things out the hard way gets you to the good way. But for the rest of you, you need to earn the right to solve a problem. Take me back to day zero, when you first believed you found a problem worth solving. In this chapter, you'll show that you understand the problem and are able to articulate it so clearly that it is undeniably true *and* important to solve—with or without you and your solution. Right now, your only job is to understand the problem deeply in all its dimensions. It's the step between "I have an idea" and "I can do something about it." It's the core thesis that your entire business will be built on. For now, ignore your solution. When you find it after you know the problem, and you will, the rest of this journey becomes so much easier, because you understand the why and what of your business. You will be able to communicate it, speaking powerfully to who your real customers are. Mastering the problem lets you see the entire journey.

And that, my friend, is how you earn the right to exist as a startup. By looking for proof before taking every single next step, you avoid automatic failure. By being smart enough to look at this objectively. Remove yourself from the solution. Inhabit the problem space. By the end of this chapter, you'll have earned the right to think about starting to solve the problem. (Chapter 4 will also delve into this in more detail.) This alone will put you miles ahead of most wannabe founders, the ones wasting time and money hiring an engineer on Upwork, racing to build a product no one wants.

Identify a Real, Painful Problem

Is your problem actually a problem? Or is it just a mild inconvenience that people can easily live with? What makes you think you can tell the difference?

Real problems are painful. They cost people or businesses significant time, money, or emotional distress. They're the kind of issues that keep your potential customers up at night, the thorns in their side that they'd *pay good money to remove*.

Take this quick test. If you don't know the answer to these questions, that's cool. Don't fake it. The point is to uncover, honestly, where you are in the problem validation process and then help you get where you need to be.

Can you describe the problem in one clear sentence (no jargon allowed)?

Will solving this problem save someone a significant amount of money? Or time?

Will solving this problem make someone a significant amount of money (other than you)?

Will solving this problem eliminate significant emotional distress or friction?

If you can't confidently answer yes to at least two of these, we need to dig a little deeper. You're going to need a little more data or investigation into the problem. Maybe you just need to think wider or adjacent or snowball. If you solve this problem, what other problems does it open for you to solve?

Let's go deeper. Be brutally honest. Take your one sentence description of the problem and follow up with what you know about

- how people are currently solving this problem (or coping with it) and

- what they are paying (money, labor, productivity cost, etc.) to solve this problem currently.

Here's a mega moment: It's called "rubber duck debugging." It's the practice of talking through your answers out loud, as if explaining them to a rubber duck. It helps you define, structure, clarify, and articulate your thoughts. And yes, if you do it in public, it makes you look extra crazy. But it works. In fact, it's so potent that we're going to revisit it later on your journey.

If you can't come up with any hard data, all good. Amazing. You're being honest. We know you've got more work to do. If you believe you know the answers, check yourself. Are they based in fact? Are they detailed? Now, play devil's advocate and argue against your own points. If you can't step outside your own bias, this book will be fun reading, but it won't help you get over yourself enough to build a successful startup.

Does the Problem Exist Beyond Your Bubble?

You think you've identified a real problem. Fab. Now prove it. Your opinion doesn't mean anything (yet). Neither does your mum's, your best friend's, or your cofounder's. You need objective, informed evidence that this problem exists in the real world, affecting real people or businesses. The number one reason startups fail (alongside all the other number one reasons) isn't a terrible product; it's founders building without truly understanding whom they're building for. Don't be that founder who launches to crickets, because you built based on assumptions and excitement, not reality.

Start with data and force yourself to do some math.

What hard numbers can you find?

How many people or businesses are affected by this problem?

What's the financial impact?

The time impact?

Don't guess. Find a source, a data point you can attach to, industry reports, academic studies, government data, or use inferred assumptions. Dig deep. Everyone hates doing this because it takes more than one Google search. It's going to take you down paths you haven't traveled before.

Here's an exercise I walk my clients through: Figure out how many eggs Americans eat every year. Use only logical deduction and some basic known facts. What did you come up with?

This exercise forces you to think critically and make reasonable assumptions. It goes from a stupid, impossible-to-answer question to a linear, obvious process of questions and answers. So much of equipping you for the founder's journey is about advancing your critical thinking.

By the way, the answer doesn't matter because it's a ridiculous question. What matters is how this question triggers your brain.

Data is epic but isn't enough. You need nuance. You think you've found the next big thing—great! But if it doesn't resonate with customers, it means nothing.

Invest real effort in customer discovery: a systematic, ongoing process to understand your prospect's problems, needs, and wants. It's not about pitching your product or validating your genius solution. It's validating your assumptions. At the same time, it is building relationships and getting real feedback from real people who could be your future customers. Don't approach customer discovery as a one-time checkbox. The real value is in perpetuating an ongoing conversation that informs and shapes every part of your business, from product to marketing and everything in between.

Customer discovery means that you need to talk to real people. Not your friends. Not your family. Strangers but not randos. People who fit the profile of your potential customers, the people you had in mind when you wrote down who is having this problem. Remember your most important goal: Build a product people want and will actually pay for.

Jobs Didn't Do It

Every founder always hits me with the classic excuse "But Steve Jobs didn't do customer discovery." First, that's a myth. Jobs was obsessed with understanding user behavior and needs. Second, you're not Steve Jobs. That's the end of the sentence!

You might think it's too early in your journey for this, but it isn't. And that's not my opinion. It's a demonstrable,

Despite what you think, your startup isn't about you or your brilliant idea. **It's about solving a real problem for real people.**

constant, universal truth. The most visionary founders are grounded in a deep understanding of their customers' needs.

You'll hear me talk a lot about getting in traffic, being in the arena, and having conversations (after conversations, after conversations). Customer discovery is the core of your entire startup journey because it should help you find customers who want to buy your product, not just use it for free or think it's a cool idea. Despite what you think, your startup isn't about you or your brilliant idea. It's about solving a real problem for real people. The only way to do that effectively is to understand those people deeply.

Which One Are You?

When it comes to customer discovery, there are two founder archetypes:

1 Vacuum founders: These product-driven founders believe their solution, feature, or function will conquer all. Talking to prospects feels uncomfortable and out of their lane. They think they can rely on their amazing product to win over customers, but it rarely works. Why? Because they never actually asked anyone what they want. Fact: Winning products and companies rarely emerge from a lone person toiling away in a basement.

2 (Trying to be) Purist founders: You're reading this, you know it's important, and you want to do it right. But without formalizing the process, you mistake words for signals and those signals for validation. Stuck in founder bias, you have lukewarm conversations that don't lead anywhere. Hearing "Let me know when it's ready" sounds

like validation, but it's not. You haven't earned the right to have a real conversation where prospects can give honest feedback.

Second-time founders don't make this mistake. They know better because they learned the hard way and usually paid the price.

Be a Brave Discoverer

Customer discovery is finding that one person, that one conversation, that one moment where you know exactly whom you're building for. It's when you start hearing the same things repeatedly, when you can predict what they'll say before they say it, when you understand their world better than they do and can solve their problems. That's the power of customer discovery.

Aside from me screaming that either you won't do it or you'll do it wrong, an effective customer discovery process ideally includes some new unaffiliated connections and is just a process that you form. Crafting and having useful conversations is an art, with the primary objective of trying to get some actual data that can be of real impact.

Now you need to make contact. Find your potential customers, start a conversation, then shut up and listen. This is harder than it sounds. Most founders can't help but pitch their idea or argue their point. But that's not what this is about. It's about understanding the pain your potential customers actually feel.

When I encourage you to talk to your potential buyers, what I mean is *listen* to them. Rule number one—and I keep a

Post-it note above my computer screen to constantly remind me of this—is "Shut the fuck up." Listen to understand, not to wait for your turn to say something clever.

Here's some guidance on how to make customer discovery deliver value for you.

Have the right mindset. You are there to learn, to understand their world, not yours. Be curious, be open, be exploratory. Look for people who you think may know (and have) the problem. You are absolutely *not* allowed to pitch your idea and your clever solution. You only want to understand their pain. The intent is *not* to get a customer; it's to gain understanding.

Ask open-ended questions. Don't be explicit ("Would you buy this product?"). Instead ask them to walk you through how they currently solve the problem: what happens before and after; what are their pain points, their happiness moments, the magic wand impact. Explain that you're researching a problem, not selling anything. "I'm trying to learn more about [the problem]. Can you tell me how you handle [this problem]? Walk me through the process. What's the most frustrating part of [the problem]? Where does the process break, get stuck, or not deliver?" Keep these questions focused on the moment/process you are trying to learn more about.

Pay attention. If you are actually listening and processing, not forming your next question or looking to show how smart you are, you will ask follow-up questions and dig deeper, especially when they say something of interest or something you don't quite understand. Practice active listening.

Watch for (nonverbal) signals. These could be tone of voice, leaning in, getting excited or passionate or fiery or anything. Nonverbal cues are always better than words. When a prospect leans in and sounds engaged, they might become an advocate on your journey. If they get defensive, is there something in your questions that suggests they are shit at their job? If they don't care about the problem because they aren't touched by the impact of failure, pay attention. Are you talking to the wrong person in the organization? Can they point you to someone else?

Make unaffiliated connections. Find new people, unimpacted by your existing circle. Cold. If you can't find anyone, aside from probably not trying hard enough, maybe that's a signal in itself.

Look for patterns. We're not searching for statistically significant data here. We're looking for patterns, for those aha moments that shift perspective. Dig deeper with the 5 Whys technique: Keep asking "Why?" to get past symptoms to the root of the problem. How they currently do it. Why? How they want it done. Why? What they tried that didn't work. Why? You get it. Keep probing to get to the root cause.

Lean into discomfort. This process is uncomfortable for most of us, especially at the beginning when you are in founder mumble mode. No one cares (yet), trust me. You'll have awkward and hard conversations and things you don't want to hear. Good, better to face the truth than to build a product no one wants. That's real pain.

Keep going. Never stop listening, learning, refining. Ever.

Get Started

To make this worthwhile, you need to create your own framework for effective potential customer interviews. Be clear on what you are looking to learn. Find your style. Respect what your prospects know. This is not an interrogation so keep witness intimidation out of it. The goal is to learn how to get valuable feedback from insiders, information you can evaluate and use to inform your decisions. This is all about protecting you from making stupid assumptions. Give it a go. You'll be terrible at first but keep at it.

Do at least twenty of these interviews. Fifty is better. One hundred is ideal. Pattern recognition is your friend, if you have the capability to see the clues and put them together. Are you hearing the same themes over and over? When you talk about the problem does it set them off? These are all signals—whether they're telling you you're right, you're wrong, or you need to refine your approach to describing the problem.

Hearing signals is an art. Reading into the answers takes practice. The more of these interviews you do, the less you mumble, the more confident you become, the more questions you answer, the more key, powerful words you pick up (insider lingo). If you do this deliberately and thoughtfully, there is no way that interview number twenty is not exponentially better than interview number one. I know this is painful, but there is literally no downside if you spend your time listening, not arguing, and not selling (yet).

Just One

One conversation away from everything changing. One insight away from unlocking that real value. One person away from finding your first customer.

This process is your training for sales, for investors, for recruits. It is so crucial to founder success that it gets its own chapter (and will be repeated every chapter) because most founders won't do it. By launch (chapter 11), you'll realize that *one extra email or conversation* could have compounded into something significant. Not only a bigger network but an engaged network that helps you when you go to market. And even more importantly, you're building the muscle memory of empathy.

Identify Your Beachhead

Interviews complete and findings analyzed, you've done the initial hard work of better understanding the problem. Now it's time to get strategic. You can't boil the ocean all at once, but you can boil one cup at a time. Identify your beachhead: the specific, narrow slice of the market where you're going to plant your flag and prove your concept.

Your answer should be close to embarrassing, close to self-deprecating, the smallest group of smalls. Stop trying to conquer the planet and impress everyone with your grand visions. You are trying to identify the most impacted, the most viable, the most *x* piece of the market.

You can't do this meaningfully without knowing your ideal customer profile (ICP). Who is experiencing this problem most acutely? Who has the biggest pain, the most to gain, and the willingness and ability to pay for a solution?

Be painfully specific. "Small businesses" isn't an ICP. "E-commerce stores with 5-20 employees with a founder in the East Coast, in business under three years, doing $1-$5 million in annual revenue, selling physical products with complex supply chains"—that's an ICP.

Now, push on. What are the psychographics of your ICP? What are their values, their attitudes towards innovation, their decision-making processes? The more you understand them, their needs and behaviors, the better you can tailor your approach. You are trying to get an early glimpse of the market for this problem (not your solution!). To get your head around the who, just taking the first steps in thinking, "*Who are we solving the problem for?*"

As you construct your ICP, consider these standard traits:

Demographics: Industry, company size, location, etc.

Firmographics: Revenue, growth rate, technology stack, etc.

Psychographics: Values, attitudes, interests, lifestyle, etc.

Behaviors: Buying patterns, decision-making processes, risk tolerance, etc.

Needs: Pain points, goals, challenges, etc.

Once you've defined your ICP, you need to think about how to reach your ideal customers. Where do they hang out online? What conferences do they attend? What publications do they read? In these early days, you are trying to paint as complete a picture of your target customer as possible.

Construct your ideal customer profile (ICP) using demographics, psychographics, behavioral characteristics, and what color car they drive (joking). You're earning the right to know exactly who your first customers are.

Quantify the Problem Impact

We think we have a problem identified, we think we have validated it to be broadly real, we think we have even figured out who these people are who may be willing to pay for the problem to go away. Great. Now we need to understand just how big a deal this problem really is.

Problem impact analysis. Sounds awful and it is. This is where you actually have to do work and math and research and things. Just in case you had this illusion of being a funtimes founder, spending a lot of time visioning and selling people on your great innovation, that role doesn't exist. A majority of your time is spent doing hard things, because the ability to stick with and finish hard things is what sets you apart from the founders who won't, can't, or don't.

So more thorny questions.

First, "What benefits will customers experience *directly* from the problem being solved?" Be specific.

"Saves time" isn't good enough. Quantify wherever possible. "Reduces contract review time by 60 percent, saving an average of 15 hours per week for legal teams" is what we're looking for.

Next, "How will fixing this problem change the size and behavior of the market?"

This is where you start to build your case for why this is a big fucking deal. Are you expanding an existing market? Creating an entirely new one? Be realistic, but don't be afraid to think big.

Then, "What broader economic impact might occur, beyond direct customer benefits?"

This is where you can really flex your understanding of the problem's ripple effects. Are there second-order consequences that could be even bigger than the immediate problem you're solving?

Finally, "Does the impact change the Only Metric That Matters (OMTM) by more than 20 percent?"

This is your North Star. If you can't move a key metric by at least 20 percent, you're probably not solving a big enough problem. Or maybe you are, but is it big enough to warrant a purchase, implementation, and all the hassle that comes with adopting a new solution? How big an impact does it have? How much pain does it relieve? Turn it into numbers.

I know. This is a lot. And it would be more fun to be writing code or haggling over design details for your landing page. Not yet. Getting smarter about the problem sets you up for the next big risk mitigator: understanding where you enter the value chain. Read on.

EARN IT

Estimate the financial or time impact of the problem for your target market. Be as specific as possible. If you can't put a number on it, you don't understand the problem well enough yet. Identify the OMTM for your potential customers and calculate how much your solution could move that metric.

4

EARN THE RIGHT TO SOLVE A PROBLEM, PART 2

I KNOW. HERE WE ARE, still talking about the damn problem. When do we get to hear about your totally brilliant, unbelievable, kickass solution? Not today.

Most people, first-time founders included, believe startups fail because they run out of money. I don't buy that. The biggest reason startups fail is that the founder is unwilling to do the grindingly slow analytical work required to become deeply informed about the problem. Desperate to have "something to show," they can't stop themselves from impulsively, compulsively building their solution before they can demonstrate anyone needs it.

Startups are a game of patience. The public glory comes from the private sacrifice, the founders who know they have to do the work, not the founder who downloads a list of investors and fires off a mass email expecting some results.

Patience is so hard to practice. It doesn't mean slow; it means hurry slowly.

My wager is this: Instead of blasting ahead now to build your prototype, hit pause. If you invest a bit more time learning all you can about your problem in its multidimensional complexity (you'll need to spend more than a minute, but it won't take months or years), then *100 percent guaranteed*, the time and energy you spend delving deep into the problem space will save you the $30,000, $60,000, or $100,000 you'd have totally wasted on your useless version 1 solution. Even more importantly, the commitment I make to you is that the time you are spending now will give you customers *before you launch*. You heard that right: the guarantee of revenue *before your product is built*. Think of this as getting paid while you investigate.

Map the Problem in Your Value Chain

This is not like either of the standard value chain approaches: the linear model that follows the creation of a product or service from supplier to buyer or the internal operations model that examines every touchpoint within your business to see where or if value is being added. What I'm framing challenges you to build a mind map of critical thinking to gain a deeper understanding of where you sit in the market and where your solution intervenes. What we're trying to understand is exactly where you fit in the flow that surrounds the problem.

Through this process, you will confront the huge disconnect that too often tragically separates *customer success* from *solution success*. Don't make that mistake. By zooming out, we're going to map out the entire journey from when your customer first realizes they have a problem to when they achieve their ultimate goal. This is known as "looking up and down the beach," a kinder, gentler way of saying "mapping the value chain."

It's sticky, so let's break this down step by step in a series of detailed questions. It helps to jot down your answers. The value chain is really tough, because it's so technical by design. But it's asking for an answer to exactly at what point your problem comes into play, and how, for whom, and when.

To get you started, because this is a hard thing to grasp for all of us, here's what a value chain can look like.

Problem Origination: What are the *root causes* that lead to this problem emerging?

Problem Development: How does the issue evolve over time?

Problem "Owners": Who are the key stakeholders affected at each stage?

Solution Intervention: Where exactly does your (still hypothetical) solution fit?

Solution Deliverables: What specific jobs does it do?

Solution Success: What are the immediate impacts and benefits of your solution?

Solution Metrics: How do you measure success?

Client Success: What's the ultimate goal for your customer? How does your solution contribute to or achieve that larger vision?

Great. Now it gets a bit more complicated. At each of the stages above, from problem origination to client success, consider your answers, taking into account these four clarifiers. Jot down your thoughts.

1 Technology: What tech is currently in use? What are its limitations?

2 Ownership: Who owns the problem at each stage versus who has the power to implement a solution?

3 Friction: What obstacles exist that could hinder adoption of a new solution?

4 Truths: What do you know to be *undeniably* true about each stage of the process? P.S. Assumptions are not welcome here.

This exercise is designed to be hard. It forces you to think holistically about the problem to enable you to surface potential roadblocks, name key decision-makers, and recognize critical integration points for your future (still hypothetical!) solution.

If you struggled to come up with answers, you're probably wondering where to go to find useful insights. Go find some people experiencing the problem. If there's no one already in your network, do a LinkedIn search. Who are your competitors? Who uses their product or service? Track these users down and chat them up. They may prove to be potential new customers of yours. Get out in the field and observe how people do shit. Ask for people willing to share their experience. You're just giving folks a chance to bitch about their pain points.

Remember, you are *listening*, not selling. Problem validation is based on continually seeking out conversations with all sorts of people who are likely to say, "That sounds amazing, but have you considered x?"

Once you begin to master this approach you will go back to it again and again. Because as any successful founder knows, this type of search is never going to end. The problem will change as the market changes and you will be trying to solve

Remember, you are listening, **not selling.**

for the unknown again to meet the evolving needs of your customer, your investor, your staff, your marketing plan—basically all of it.

Let me be clear, I am not proposing that you'll find all your answers by talking to potential customers. The need for a new solution or the solution itself is often not recognized by the users. That said, what if all your conversations and research do not validate your view of the problem? Maybe you are the only one who sees it clearly. You have to ask yourself, "Am I a visionary or am I delusional?" and there can be a very thin line separating the two. Don't hide behind your confirmation bias. Keep communicating with people who ask tough questions. As a founder, you have to determine early on that the problem you've identified has significant market value. And that judgment must be based on more than a gut feeling. You don't have to look far to find the wreckage of companies built on "problem solutions" no one wanted.

Only when you truly understand where you live in the ecosystem does your problem become real. Ideally, you've defined a problem worth spending money on (if not, it's a great time to bail and find a "better" problem). Describing an undeniably real problem helps you map out your stakeholders: the buyers, the users, all the people impacted.

Prove You Understand the Problem

By now, you should understand the problem better than when we started. It's impossible you didn't learn and iterate as a result of your exploration. This is a huge part of the journey. Before you build, you will be on version 50 of this idea, having made forty-nine tweaks to make your solution better and more likely to win. Compare that to the founder who hired a bunch of folks and jumped into building their big idea: They're still on version 1, burning cash and building the wrong thing for nobody.

Once you've truly understood the problem, you should be able to articulate it better than your potential customers can. You learned how to describe it from listening to them. Mimic their words. But to make sure you've got it right, ask your potential users or the people you have spoken to how they would describe your solution. These have to be nonaffiliated people—no one in your circle or anyone vested in your success. It's some sampling of people, more than one. If you can get 500, great. If you get ten, that's okay too. Some of you will go to founder meetups. Others will put their problem into the ether and post it on Reddit. It's about getting feedback that is real and represents the customers who are going to end up buying your solution.

Now you can do something concrete (finally!). Create a simple landing page or a one-pager that describes the problem. No solutions. No features. No benefits. Just a clear, compelling description of the problem and its impact. Congratulations! You have the first web presence of your product.

Hopefully, you have already registered your web domain and all the social handles with consistent verbiage. You've got an attractive but inexpensive logo from Fiverr or such. Maybe you've got an image for a landing page "designed" to showcase the problem. Your first web presence is more about being forced to work out how to describe everything in a five-word headline followed by a fifteen-word sentence of explanation. *Not of what your product does but of the problem it solves and the outcome your users will get.* This is the difference between founders who talk about their features versus the founders who talk about the pain their prospective customers have. In a way, the landing page is symbolic. It's for you, to calm your anxiety about not having anything to show. It may not be much, but your business idea just got real.

Poke some holes in your statement. What are the top five questions or objections you expect to hear from your ICP about this problem? Then go out and have more conversations. How close were your predictions? The better you anticipate your ICP's thoughts and concerns, the more deeply you understand the problem.

If you're feeling frustrated, confused, or like you're going in circles, good. That's normal. Understanding a problem deeply enough to build a business around it is hard work. Embrace the fact that the founder's journey is a loop, repeating a process again and again, so that you just incrementally keep moving forward. Maybe only 1 percent at a time.

But here's the thing: Every conversation, every iteration, every moment of doubt is making you smarter about this problem. You're building the foundation for every single thing that comes next. At this stage, *you're not trying to be right. You're trying to be less wrong.* Each step done honestly reduces uncertainty. It lets you understand a problem in ways that resonate with your potential customers. And as if that weren't reason enough, this exercise compounds the work you did to map your value chain. Specifically, these difficult practices do the following:

- Save you from chasing ghosts and phantom opportunities.
- Stop you from building a solution to a problem that nobody cares about.
- Unlock hidden markets. Problem exploration reveals problems you might not have considered, bigger frictions, and potentially untapped markets.

- Strengthen your investor pitch dramatically. A real problem statement with data to back it up demonstrates your deep understanding of the *actual* market.

Build Your Problem Thesis

You've done the research. You've validated the pain. You've mapped the ecosystem. You've identified your beachhead. Now it's time to pull it all together into a cohesive problem thesis.

This is your master document, your cheat sheet, the one document that has all the stuff.

Your problem thesis should be a clear, compelling argument for why this problem needs to be solved, why now is the right time to solve it, and why the market is ready for a new solution.

It should include the following:

- a clear, concise statement of the problem (you already have that!)

- quantifiable evidence of the problem's impact and market size (you did that work too)

- an explanation of why existing solutions are inadequate (got it)

- a description of your ICP and why these customers are the right initial target (nailed it)

- your hypothesis on the key elements required for a successful solution (How will you overcome the friction and objections?)

You don't have to look far to find the wreckage of **companies built on "problem solutions" no one wanted.**

This thesis becomes your North Star. It guides your product development, your go-to-market strategy, your pitch to investors. It's the foundation upon which you'll build your entire startup. This, my friend, is why we took so much time to get to this huge milestone in your founder's journey.

The Final Test, for Now

If you made it here, kudos! I asked you to take so many steps you probably hated or thought were a huge fucking waste of time. But I swear, *executing every one of these steps will save you months or years of building something no one wants.* Which brings us to the next big hurdle.

Can you sell the problem? *Not* your solution. The problem.

If you can demonstrate you're able to do this, you've proven at least in a small way there's a real, painful problem that people are willing to pay to solve. You've laid the groundwork for a startup that has a fighting chance. It's not so binary. We want it to be but it's not. That's why I keep urging you to get into traffic, speak to people, get some feedback, keep at it. I know it's really hard, but you have to work out how you are speaking to the market and keep adjusting. It's harder but far more effective than building an entire solution and then presenting it as "done."

I hear the opposing viewpoint: "Customers don't know what they want until you do it." Or the outright naysayers tell you you're nuts, like the "wise ones" who unequivocally told Airbnb founders, "No one wants to rent out a room in their house to a random stranger over the internet." You've got a choice to make if "No way" is all you're hearing. Worst case, it's better to find out now before you've sunk months or years of your life into building a solution nobody wants. Another option: Are you going to close the laptop, pack up, and go home? Or defiantly claim, "No one understands, but in time they'll see I'm right"? Before you do, consider this.

I know it sounds bizarre, but falling in love with the problem, not the solution, is what separates successful founders from the dreamers. It's what earns you the right to even think about solving it. It's what will guide you through the inevitable pivots and challenges ahead. Go back and get the problem right before you quit and definitely before you build.

So there you have it. You've earned the right to solve a problem. We didn't once mention your startup, your solution—not once. You're pointed in the right direction, heading for your North Star, and that's a really great place to be.

EARN IT

Find five people who fit your ICP.

Pitch them the problem.

Tell them you're thinking about starting a company to solve this issue, but *before* you do, you want to make sure you really understand the problem.

Ask them (this takes courage) if they'd be willing to pay for a solution *if* you could deliver one that truly solved their pain points.

If you can get three out of five to say some variations of "tell me more" or "I might be interested" or even "yes," big congratulations! You've earned the right to start thinking about solutions.

5

EARN THE RIGHT TO ENTER THE MARKET

IF YOU'RE still with me, it means that despite every honest attempt to argue, find cracks, and compete with your own bias, you still think you have a problem worth solving. Epic. May you never lose that underlying absolute conviction in your vision. Now, before you build a thing, you need to prove you have the right to even attempt to solve it, a right to enter the market.

How do you earn that right?

First, you've got to truly understand the battlefield you're about to step onto. Because that's what it is: a battlefield. You're taking a dollar from someone else's revenue stream. Rarely is no one negatively impacted by your success. When you think about the market and all the wisdom you might have, start by forgetting everything (especially the many assumptions) you think you know. Unless of course you're already the dominant leader in this industry, which, let's face it, you're probably not. Yet.

The right to enter the market comes from proving you have a place in it. Showing you can make an impact. Demonstrating you can build a business that is actually worth something. The process of proving it means moving away from being a dreamer with a laptop and a latte into the much more demanding stance of being a CEO who understands how they're going to propel this idea into the market.

Everything about this chapter will challenge your dreams as it asks you to rise up and give those dreams a fighting chance in the real world. If you can't communicate it, you can't manifest it. It's time to take your spark of an idea and turn it into a real, viable *business*. Rightly or wrongly, we've accepted that you've found a problem worth solving, but can it become a *business*? What you uncover next might require us to take your idea and move it a little, pivot a little, fight a little, or change a lot.

Red Ocean or Blue Ocean?

When you begin evaluating your market, think strategically about where you fit in. Are you building into a red ocean or a blue one? In reality, the marketplace is all one ocean, but it's a way of framing your idea to understand at least broadly the level of competition and resistance you will face.

Red oceans are existing markets. They're crowded and competitive, with established players and clear rules of engagement. The mechanics and economics of the business are predefined (not to say you can't change them). If, for example, you want to build a new CRM, you're diving into a pretty busy market with some heavyweight players. That's a red ocean. Entering a red ocean requires you to differentiate yourself clearly and compellingly *right away*. If what you're offering is merely an "iteration" of the existing options, it's probably not going to be enough. You'll find yourself fighting for people to switch to you, a hard choice that needs to be worth the pain of change, no matter the price point.

Blue oceans are uncontested market spaces. They offer the opportunity to create new demand from new customers, rather than fighting over existing customers. This sounds great, right? A total white space. But here's the catch: Blue oceans are hard. You're not just selling a product. You are often creating an entirely new category. To do that, you're going to have to spend an enormous amount of time, energy, and money convincing people of this new way and why they have to have it.

There's nothing wrong with either approach. In fact, I often advocate for founders to find a tiny crack, a vertical, an overlooked niche in the red ocean. Then, when you have sufficient scale, capital, or traction, you can swim across to the new market in blue waters. Generally speaking, if you want to change the world, it is best to start where you can quickly be most effective.

While we've discussed red and blue oceans as distinct concepts, the reality is that all markets exist in one fluid ecosystem: It's one big ocean. The key is not to obsess over whether you're in a red or blue ocean but to find your unique position within the broader market. Your goal is to create a space where your strengths align perfectly with customer needs, regardless of how crowded or open that initial space may seem.

This allows for a more nuanced approach to market entry. Instead of trying to categorize your entire market as red or blue and categorize yourself, focus on identifying specific opportunities where you can create unique value. These opportunities might exist in pockets of uncontested space within an otherwise crowded market or in unexplored areas adjacent to existing markets.

A blue ocean today might be red tomorrow.

Analyze your market. Is it a red ocean or a blue ocean? List three key competitors (for red oceans) or three potential barriers to adoption (for blue oceans). Then, challenge yourself to explain in one paragraph how you plan to differentiate yourself or create demand for your new category. In the end, there's really only one ocean...

Understanding Your Market: Size Matters

Now that we've framed the competitive landscape, how big is the opportunity? After all, knowing which ocean is only half the battle—you also need to know how big that ocean is.

How big is your intended market? As in, if you owned 100 percent market share, where absolutely everyone who needed this thing bought it from you, how many people would that represent?

A hard question to answer, but one you need to figure out, even vaguely. The truth is no one knows for certain. But let's see if we can at least convincingly indicate that it's *big*. Big enough to be worthwhile or big enough to warrant outside investment or big enough to be a great small "lifestyle" business for you.

We can break downsizing the market into three key concepts, each progressively more narrow and well defined, like a pyramid turned upside down.

1. Total Addressable Market (TAM): This is everyone in the world who could theoretically use your product or service. It's the big, ridiculous, fantasy number, but the math is not "not real."

    Example: You're building a new productivity app for freelancers. Your TAM might be all freelancers worldwide. That's a big number, but it's not very realistic.

2. Serviceable Addressable Market (SAM): This is the portion of the TAM that you can *realistically* reach with your current business model and technology. It's smaller than the TAM but still ambitious.

    Example: For your freelancer app, your SAM might be English-speaking freelancers in the specific countries where you can effectively market and support your product.

3. Serviceable Obtainable Market (SOM): This is the portion of your SAM that you can *realistically* capture in the next three to five years. *This is the number you should care about right now.*

    Example: Your SOM might be a specific niche of freelancers (e.g., graphic designers) in certain geographic regions (e.g., the western US) where you plan to focus your initial marketing efforts.

It doesn't matter if your market seems a touch small. Better to be believable than boastful. There are always adjacent markets, and it's also why the True Total Addressable Market (TTAM) exists. The TAM you present to investors is inflated. Your TTAM is a more refined number that you know to be true.

But here's the mess with market size—it's not just about how big it is. It's about finding your place in it. That's where the power of niche comes in.

Humor Me

Trying to land a joke in these tense times is like walking onto a minefield. Yet we could all use a good laugh, especially in stressful situations. Like when pitching to angel investors.

A client of mine told me how she used humor to win over a skeptical audience of angels. Her business centered on providing services to small businesses across the Middle East, a region notoriously sketchy on reliable market data. Estimating the size of her potential market was going to take creative math. She knew it and so did the angels in the room. Her solution was to play with their expectations.

"I know you're all eager to see the size of the market for my services," she began, then she clicked on a slide that simply read "HUGE." Everyone in the room laughed out loud. The next slide laid out her "back of napkin" math, but it almost didn't matter because she had eased the way for acceptance.

A rule of thumb for angel approval is to convince 60 to 70 percent of the audience. She scored 100 percent and raised $1 million. It wasn't just humor. She attributed her success to three factors:

- a clean, easy-to-follow slide deck
- telling a story, not just reading the slides
- using humor to connect with the humanity of the audience

Crafting a good joke takes work and thought. It can't be snarky. It can't make others look bad. It can't be intended to puff you up. It can arise from knowing what your audience is thinking and expecting, and surprising them while maybe taking a poke at yourself. Employed in moderation and with tact, humor is a powerful and often underused force.

The Power of Niche

You see the point here, right? We're trying to find the tiniest of niches, places in the market where you might be able to open up a crack and get some traction. So many founders make the mistake of shooting too broadly, but it doesn't work. Trying to build something for everyone usually results in building nothing for no one. Or something too few people want.

Founders often resist the advice to be vertical-specific on their website. They worry that stating who they serve will limit their opportunities or make them seem too small and unattractive to attract potential talent. But that's the whole secret: Go as niche as you possibly can. This entire chapter is guiding you towards one thing: finding where you can win as quickly as possible.

Do we want to win for real or parade around as if we were winning?

Think about it this way: In a crowded market, being a generalist makes you invisible. Being a specialist makes you indispensable. Your niche is your superpower. It's what allows you to deeply understand your customers, speak their language, and solve their specific problems better than anyone else. If you nail it for a graphic designer, they tell another graphic designer—they don't tell a doctor. If you nail it for a graphic designer and are focused on their use case, your software becomes more and more powerful for the graphic designer. Sure, at some point you can expand out, just not today. It's much easier to grow outward from a position of strength than to exhaust yourself and your resources trying to be everything to everyone from the start.

Identify the smallest, most specific market segment where your solution can have an outsized impact. Name it.

Who are these people?

What industry are they in?

What specific, real, painful problem do they have that you can solve better than anyone?

Don't worry about the niche seeming too small. Worry about it being too broad.

Remember, Amazon started by just selling books. Facebook began as a social network for college students. Uber initially focused on black car services in San Francisco. They didn't try to boil the entire ocean from day one. They found their niche, dominated it, and then expanded.

This approach isn't just about focus—it's about survival. In the early days of your startup, resources are scarce. You can't afford to spread yourself thin trying to please everyone. By focusing on a niche, you can concentrate your limited resources for maximum impact.

As we continue through this chapter, keep asking yourself, "Where can I win? What's the smallest market where I can make the biggest impact?" That's how you earn the right to enter the market. That's how you start building a business that matters.

The Atomic ICP

Let's assume, for now, you agree with me, and you are willing to narrow down your market and go full-on niche. Just for a second, dig deeper into that niche, because this is where your ideal customer hangs out. Your incredibly important ICP.

The ICP is the smallest, most specific, most powerful subset of customers who are absolutely perfect for your product. One key element that makes them perfect is their *capability to buy*. In general, the buyer and the user of a product are often different, especially in larger organizations, where you are likely to find a manager buying for an employee, a team lead buying for the organization, IT buying for the organization. You need to figure out who is who.

When we think about the ICP initially, for the purpose of simplicity, it helps us to consider the buyer and the user as the same person. We need them to have the budget or hold a credit card. Most likely we need them to be at a company small enough that making a purchasing decision does not demand a full-scale security audit or full-suite integrations. In this exercise, we are trying to get rid of all the buyers in your head that you love, all the imagined customers you want, and replace them with the *customer you can actually have*. This is the customer so desperate to have their problem solved that you can pitch them, and they will close the deal.

Which leads us to the Atomic ICP, the person we so deeply and so clearly understand. This is not "a twenty-five-year-old graphic designer with three years' experience, a few customers, and $15,000 a month in revenue." Your Atomic ICP is a *person* with defining traits, unmet needs, habits, and expectations. Your ICP is not a logo. It is the individual who feels the pain, has the authority to decide, and is perfectly aligned with your solution's capability to address their own specific, pressing needs. This is your target, the person fully capable of conversion from prospect to buyer. Your Atomic ICP is a very specific *person* we'll call John. Once we know this, everything we build into, market, message, architect is around John.

Getting to this level of understanding gives you a much better chance of gaining traction instead of spinning your wheels. Once you know everything about John, he has a seat at the table, going right along with you on your founder's journey.

Here's an example of an Atomic ICP based on owners of small recruiting firms with fewer than twenty-five employees. In these firms, the owner was the CEO, actively engaged and with a decent web presence (that is, vaguely familiar with the internets). We recognized these owners were entrepreneurial, so they were likely to give another founder the time of day. They have an American Express card in their back pocket, can make a decision and pay immediately, and are very likely to see the time-saving aspect and impact of our software on their bottom line and improved customer value.

What does John do in any given week? See how well you know him by mapping his activities for a typical day, from the moment he wakes up to the moment he goes to sleep.

Ecosystem Mapping

What nine-letter word accelerates customers, useful intelligence, valuable features, acquisition, retention, and credibility? You used to think the answer was "investors." But soon you'll know it's "ecosystem." If you're a bootstrapper, this method is your lifesaver. If you're already cash fantastic, here's your booster rocket.

Your startup doesn't exist in a vacuum. You're part of a complex ecosystem of customers, competitors, partners, and influencers. Understanding this ecosystem is crucial to your success. No matter your industry, the existing market is so competitive you must know who currently sells to your ICP, who understands their needs and processes better than you do, and who wields actual influence over your customers. That's your ecosystem. It's going to take some smart fighting to fit into it, but without a strategy, you can't accomplish what you need to make it happen: becoming plainly visible and easily accessible to the customers who want or need what you have to offer.

This is a very functional process (not much fun or fluff here) that starts by identifying all of the key players.

Direct competitors: Who's solving the same problem you are?

Indirect competitors: Who's solving adjacent problems or offering alternative solutions?

Potential partners: Who could amplify your reach or complement your offering?

Key influencers: Who shapes opinions in your space?

Gatekeepers: Who controls access to your potential customers?

Customers: Who are you serving and who influences their decisions?

Suppliers: Who provides critical components or services for your offering?

Regulatory bodies: Who sets the rules in your industry?

Think about how all these players interact. Who has the power? Who's vulnerable? Where are the opportunities for collaboration? Where are the potential threats? Where are the blockers?

An ecosystem map reveals who everyone is and who has a hand in making your solution successful. You will begin to understand who wants to keep you out, who can let you in, who is going to love you or hate you. Much of what you have been asked to do so far in your founder's journey has been an individual effort. But ultimately, building a successful enterprise is *never* a solo venture, despite the bogus claims of some "self-made" entrepreneurs. Take a closer look and you'll see the transformative power of tapping into an ecosystem behind every successful venture.

Founders who are stuck in small-scale thinking only explore their ecosystem to identify who else can *sell* their product. That's surely part of the potential play, but there's a great deal more short, mid-range, and long-term value accessible through multiple aspects of your ecosystem.

Some ecosystem activating moves you can make are as follows:

Leverage your existing resources and networks to speed growth and establish differentiation.

Integrate with others' systems to enhance your product's appeal and stickiness.

Access new markets through strategic partnerships and new channels.

Align with industry leaders to benefit from market influence and build competitive advantage.

Consider these nine areas of ecosystem opportunity you should mine for gold.

1. Outbound marketplace: Increase visibility and customer access by increasing the number of platforms where your app is listed for exposure, purchase, and direct integration in a marketplace with other applications or services. For example, your software as a service (SaaS) tool is available

in Salesforce AppExchange, making it easily accessible to businesses.

2   Inbound marketplace: Create a hub or feature within your product that hosts a range of third-party apps or services for integration to add value to your customers. Invite innovation and see the value of your platform increase. An example would be a marketplace where users can single-click to integrate with their existing stack.

3   Channel: Form partnerships with resellers, affiliates, distributors, and others who (help) sell your product to their established customer base or whose reputation adds shine to your credibility in the market. For example, align with consultants who can package your product, resell your product, or leverage trust among their client base to drive adoption of your product.

4   Implementation: Identify possible partners already in your customers stack who can implement, configure, or enable customers to adopt and integrate your software efficiently. An example would be partnering with IT consultancies that specialize in deploying your software in enterprise environments.

5   Globalization and localization: Consider how reasonable adaptations of your startup's offerings will enable it to meet international standards, enter new markets, and conform to local expectations. For example, collaborate with regional partners in Asia or elsewhere to localize, sell, and support your app in their territory.

6   Indirect revenue: Generate indirect revenue by monetizing aspects of your product or user base indirectly, such

as through data partnerships or other channels. An example would be partnering with a research firm that uses aggregate, anonymized data from your users to generate industry insights.

7. Direct (non-core) income: Unlock additional income from ancillary services or features that are not your primary product but are related to and valued by your customer's ecosystem. An example would be offering in-platform ads, affiliate or other for-sale services by third parties of interest to the user.

8. White/gray label: Look for opportunities for your solution to be rebranded by another company, as a standalone offering or in partnership. This is especially useful when there is an intermediary between you and the user base, allowing you to scale into the partner's market presence discreetly. For example, find a larger platform willing to incorporate your service into their site under their branding.

9. Accelerators: In virtually every industry, there are corporate or industry-specific accelerators that provide resources, mentorship, and access to their networks. Fast-track growth by applying to companies or programs that offer capital, mentorship, and, of lasting value, an extensive network aligned with your industry. For example, apply for admission to a healthcare accelerator that offers direct introductions to major hospitals and clinics, and has healthcare mentors and deep industry experience.

Rather than single-mindedly looking for ecosystem players who can sell your stuff, a smart engagement with others in your orbit can bring multiple rewards. Faster validation of product-market fit. Optimization of resources by using established infrastructures already in play. Greater credibility that eases market entry. And a really big one: increased investment appeal by showing strategic linkages across your industry ecosystem. That's CEO thinking in action.

When you're mapping your ecosystem, don't just think about who can help you *sell*. Think about who can help you learn, grow, and scale. The overlooked ecosystem players, the ones you won't consider partners because they can't actually just "sell your shit," often have something you don't have: access to customers who trust them. In this case, your non-selling partner might connect you to their audience who are much, much more likely to respond to your shitty outreach email.

One final note on looking for people to sell for you. No one is excited to make money selling your software. The money is in the high-quality services you provide, the innovation you deliver, the trust in and around your solution. The tired proposition that "you can make *x* dollars if you just take my product to your customers" is DOA (yeah, dead on arrival).

Maybe we can chat up players in more potentially productive areas, such as the following:

Industry analysts: They might not be customers, but they influence buying decisions and can provide valuable insights into market trends. Surely, we should introduce ourselves, explain what we are doing, and humbly ask their opinion of the market, space, and opportunity based on their deep, wide, and well-respected career in this sector.

Academics: Universities are often overlooked goldmines of research, talent, and potential partnerships. There is always a PhD student somewhere doing a thesis on something that may be key.

Sellers of complementary products: Look for products that aren't direct competitors but serve the same customer base. Who else is in the same stack that sells to your customer? Whom in this space could you play nice with?

Online communities: Forums, Reddit, LinkedIn groups—these are where your potential customers are already hanging out and discussing their problems. Get in the conversation and listen.

Former employees of competitors: They have insider knowledge of the industry, sometimes an ax to grind or a score to settle, but also maybe they like to talk about what they know. Ask them to chat. You don't want the dirt; you want to know what they did really well, what other opportunities are out there, the stuff only insiders know. Skip the office gossip. You don't care if Frank is a shitty manager (except maybe to make you feel better about yourself).

Who else can you think of who may be a super resource for you?

Update Everyone, Because Nobody Likes Surprises (Really)

Here's a small activity with big rewards as you transform yourself from a completely hopeless CEO to a great one: Learn to write to your investors. Yeah, there is the terror of facing the blank page. What do you have to say? How honest should you be about what's going on? How often do you need to share news? All legit questions.

Something founders rarely realize is that you are your first, largest, and most engaged investor. You occupy all the board seats. You own all the assets. You have a responsibility to hold yourself accountable. Taking time at the end of every week to write down what has happened, good and bad, teaches you how to think about your business. Start by doing this for yourself. But pretty soon, start sending it regularly to other people whom you want on your journey: cofounders, founding team members, potential or actual investors, mentors, key stakeholders.

Sending it to other people gets you to focus on the OMTM. You can't send them a fluff piece. You have to sharpen your ability to articulate your business, have a true handle on your metrics, vocalize your challenges, and place some bets on the future. You get to tell the story of your startup, show your commitment to driving it forward, and most of all, build trust and strengthen relationships as you ask for help and support especially in times when the news is not so good.

Committing to this practice early in your entrepreneurial journey offers great returns. Weekly updates are a powerful tool for self-assessment and planning. They enable you to check your progress against your road map and adjust as you acquire new insights. But it only works if you are honest. This applies to all aspects of your business: key performance indicators (KPIs), sales funnel, wins, and setbacks. Be mindful of confidentiality concerns and the need for realistic positivity (no wishful-thinking cheerleading). Avoid surprises by preparing your readers as situations develop.

The best way to manage this process is to jot things down during the week, make notes as things happen when possible, and dedicate time weekly to organize your thoughts into succinct, clear statements. No one expects you to be a great novelist. What matters most is that your updates follow the same consistent format, are brief, convey significant information, and arrive at the same time every week or month.

Delivering regular progress reports helps level up your CEO communication skills: you're practicing transparency, sharing your wins, and identifying areas you need help with.

Domain Expert

As if all this isn't asking enough of you, founder, you also need to become the go-to expert in your niche, the SME. Fast. You do not want to find yourself on a call with a prospect saying dumb stuff. You have to demonstrate that you know their industry, the workflows, the lingo, the buzz. This means going beyond a superficial understanding of your immediate competitors and customers and partners. You need a deep, nuanced understanding of the entire industry landscape. What are the trends? What is changing? Where are the stressors? Where are the wins? Okay, you're going to have to be a bit of a charlatan at first, but you're committed to being a quick study and to paying close attention to every new info nugget you hear.

The key to acquiring this deep and broad industry knowledge is to have probing conversations with as many experienced people as possible. Each call, each interaction is an opportunity to learn a phrase, a concept, an insider fact that you can then incorporate into your own language.

One of my clients initially described his platform as taking "job specifications" and converting them to job descriptions. On the second call he made to an ICP, he casually said, "When we do the intake from our clients." Damn. From now on whenever my client spoke about his platform he said "intake," never "job specs." This insight changed his website, email, and the conversations he had with each ICP. Using the language of experts gives you some of the expert's cred.

Almost no one does this, but... create a state of the industry report for your own use. Who are the key players? What are the recent trends? What's the future look like? Who is winning and who is losing? Why? Dig deep to truly understand your market.

Hustle Starting Now: Your 5-5-5 Plan

I get it. Like truly. The thought of putting yourself out there, talking about your barely formed idea to complete strangers, is fucking terrifying. It's you, alone, stepping out from behind your computer screen, armed with nothing but a figment of your imagination. It's ludicrous, ego bruising, and humbling.

Welcome to a world of doubt, ghosting, and rejection. You'll craft that first cold email, and it'll suck, so you will procrastinate for a ridiculous amount of time. No one wants to send an awful email. You'll rewrite it 900 times, and it'll still suck, but you actually have no idea, because you haven't tested it yet. Maybe it's amazing. Maybe your recipients can feel your passion, your commitment, your truth. The whole outreach process is awful.

But—*you have to start now.*

It's math. If your solution goes live in twelve weeks, and you're talking to, say, five new people a week (we'll get to that), that's a grand total of sixty people you'll have spoken to by launch. Sixty. That's it. That's your entire network, your potential first customers, your early adopters, your feedback loop. Sixty. Nearly nada. Surely, if that number was 120, you'd have a higher chance of more people converting from indifferent to interested. At 240, you get a higher chance of more feedback that informs (and improves) your product. By 480, it's likely someone will know someone that can probably help with something incredible that fixes something. Some might call this "luck," but truly, it's just math.

So, if you don't start now, if you keep hiding behind your laptop, tweaking your nonexistent product, you know how many people you'll have spoken to by launch? Zero. Because you are obsessing over your *product*. Real founders at this moment are obsessing over *distribution*. They are out there talking, listening, and doing something about it.

This 5-5-5 plan isn't just about building a customer base. It's about building you. It's about learning how to talk about yourself and your idea without sounding like an idiot. It's about asking for something—time, feedback, maybe even money—without feeling like you're begging. Most importantly, it's about shutting the fuck up and learning to listen.

Is it a clusterfuck? Absolutely. Will you feel like you're stumbling around in the dark? You bet. But every conversation, every question you can't answer, every awkward silence, every unanswered email is a step forward. It's all part of the process of turning that figment of your imagination into something real.

So, maybe, this can be a plan: the 5-5-5 commitment.

Five Cold Outreaches a Day

Reach out to five potential customers *every single day*, not just when you feel like it. This isn't about selling. It's about learning. Ask about their problems, current solutions, and frustrations.

Here's the kicker: Your understanding of who these people are will evolve. At first, you might be shooting in the dark. That's okay. Talking to the "wrong" person won't kill you. As you learn more about your market and refine your ICP, your outreach will get more targeted. It's all part of the process. You cannot *not* learn something by doing this. Or as I like to say, you will not be dumber after doing this.

Always better to be a giver, **not just a taker.**

Personalization is key. Do not cheat. You can use automation, sure, to improve your writing efforts but not to do it all for you. Do your research. Be intentional and show it. Let them know you've put in the effort. Or cheat like you are thinking about doing and just buy a list of 10,000 contacts, send them all your shitty automated email campaign, and sit back and wait for the seven pathetic responses that will trickle in.

Play the long game, the patience game. First-time founders have been led to expect immediate wins. Real winners know it's the output of the work that delivers the win.

Five Conversations a Week

Convert those cold outreaches into real conversations. Dive deep and really listen. Your goal is to understand their world so well that you can articulate their problems better than they can. Remember, these conversations aren't static. As you learn more about your market, your questions will evolve. You might start broad, asking about general pain points in their industry. But as you refine your focus, you'll dig into specifics about workflows, tools, and frustrations.

Record these conversations (with permission). You'll pick up on nuances you missed in the moment, and you'll have a goldmine of quotes and insights to refer back to.

Five Follow-ups to Feedback

For every bit of feedback you get, follow up with five people who gave you feedback. Show them you're listening and iterating based on what they tell you. It's way better to follow up quickly than to wait 120 days when you finally go live and send them a "Hey, we spoke three months ago. Try my product."

It's in this relationship-building that the magic happens if you let it. You're not just gathering information. You're building a community around your product (and you) before your product even exists. These early contacts aren't just potential customers. They're potential advisors, evangelists, investors, and maybe even future team members. When you go live, they are five more people who will click Like on your LinkedIn announcement. You could even tag them in the announcement and thank them. Why not? Always better to be a giver, not just a taker.

Keeping It All Together

The key to making this work is maintaining these relationships over time. Set up a system to manage these contacts. This could be a CRM, an email list, a community platform, or even just a well-organized spreadsheet. The tool doesn't matter as much as the habit.

Remember, you're playing the long game here. These relationships you're building now could be the difference between success and failure down the line. You can't possibly put a value on these relationships, so handle them with care. You'll need to store and note and tag and organize well, know your last reach-out date, know what happened in that conversation. Stop believing your brain is the appropriate place to remember nuance and manage all this intel.

Embracing the Iteration

No denying it. This process is messy. It's iterative. Your understanding of your market, your product, even your own capabilities will shift and evolve with every conversation. You might start out thinking you're building a tool for one group, only to realize three weeks in that your real market is another. That's not failure—that's progress. You are getting smarter about your market.

Your ecosystem map? It's going to change. Your market size calculations? They'll shift. Your niche focus? It might pivot. And that's all okay. In fact, it's exactly what should happen. Every no gets you closer to a yes. Every rejection teaches you something. And every conversation, no matter how awkward, is making you a better founder.

This isn't just busywork, I swear. This is you earning the right to build your product. This is you laying the foundation for your entire business. This is you investing in yourself. It doesn't make it less awful, but I hope I've convinced you to at least give it a try.

It. Never. Ends.

You're probably feeling like I'm throwing you around, up and down, being clear then not clear. But that's the point. We're trying to lay as solid a foundation as we can to enter the market, but the conditions are always shape-shifting. Customers change, markets change, competition changes. So it's a moment-in-time lay of the land. Your job (yes, another one) is to never stop learning, never stop investigating, never stop listening, and, to the best of your ability, never stop talking with prospects. In fact, that's the whole chapter: *Never stop talking to people, the right people.*

What success looks like right now is that you started this chapter with a broadly validated idea, and you've ended with a *validated market opportunity*. We know how big it is (kinda), we know the ICP (kinda), we've tested it (kinda), we've started to formulate how this might actually be *a thing*.

The final point here, a little brutal, is this: Those conversations with prospects, which I know were awful, and you probably didn't do enough of—when you go live, the people you speak to now *will be your first customers, your loudest voices, your biggest advocates*. Even if you were a mumbling muppet when you first started building these relationships. They will want you to win *because they will have been on the journey with you*. This is their product too. They will have a sense of ownership, even partnership.

You cannot see it now. I know you are fighting against me, making excuses to not talk to people because you have nothing to show. But I can guarantee you that you will, without question, wish you talked to more people and kept them close to you even when you did not always see where you were going.

When you are about to go live and are asking for those first customers, first case studies, first testimonials—these are your go-to people. They will be there for you.

EARN IT: YOUR 5-5-5 CHALLENGE

Implement the 5-5-5 plan for one week. That's five cold outreaches a day, five conversations, and five follow-ups. Every week.

Keep a record of every interaction. What did you learn? How did it change your understanding of your customer and your market?

At the end of the week, write a one-page reflection. How has your perspective shifted? What surprised you? What's your biggest takeaway?

6

EARN THE RIGHT TO AVOID CHASING PRODUCT-MARKET FIT

EITHER TODAY or at some point, the term PMF will land in your lingo. It stands for "product-market fit."

PMF is the holy grail of startups, the elusive ideal that all founders are eternally looking for (anxiously), on their way to looking for (arrogantly), or have found (delusionally).

Here's a hard truth: Everyone's chasing it, few understand it, and even fewer achieve it.

May as well face it at this stage of your journey. PMF is not a thing, but it is a thing. It's a paradox, a moving target, a moment impossible to will into existence. You'll hear fledgling founders throw around PMF-based claims, boasting, "We have found PMF," as if it's something they uncovered. Or worse, "We're on our way to PMF," like it's a destination in Google Maps.

If you're looking for PMF, you're already doing it wrong. No matter how hard you search, PMF isn't something you discover. It finds you. But only when you're too busy solving real problems for real customers to notice PMF happening.

How do you define something as nearly mythical as PMF? Here's my fave: PMF is like teenage sex. Everyone talks about it, nobody really knows how to do it, everyone thinks everyone else is doing it, so everyone claims they're doing it. My cynicism is not dismissal. Far from it. PMF matters a lot. It's just not what you think it is, and it sure as hell doesn't work the way most people think it does (much like teenage sex).

The magic that is PMF happens when you are so in tune with your market that you're solving problems your customers didn't even know they had until you showed up. It's when your product is so good, so necessary, that people can't imagine going back to life before it. It's when your biggest problem is not drumming up business but keeping up with demand. PMF is when the winds have changed direction from stubborn headwinds to glorious tailwinds. Suddenly you are sailing.

Why talk about PMF now when you don't even have a product? Because now is the time you are most vulnerable to thinking you have to chase it. You're most likely to be seduced by the false promise that finding PMF early is every startup's guarantee of success. You will have to get there eventually, but the route to PMF is by *building something so fucking good* that PMF has no choice but to find you.

Don't despair. There are signposts for the route to follow. Every founder who's made it will tell you the holy trinity of markers is customer obsession, feedback, and observability.

Everything else is noise, including whatever messages are urging you to go searching for PMF.

The PMF Mirage

Locating PMF, like finding the oasis in a desert, is a relentless, evolving, endless chase. Deceptive positive data is like shimmering signs of water on the horizon—not to be trusted. Most founders mistake early-adopter enthusiasm for true market fit. They're confusing vitamins with painkillers. You can be in revenue, have happy customers, and have growth. All without PMF.

Here's the kicker that most founders miss: Love isn't enough. Mark Zuckerberg nailed it when he broke down the stages of product development: Build a thing, get people to love that thing, make sure people come back to the thing, monetize the thing.

Let that sink in for a moment. Love and retention are not the same thing. Your users may love your product, rave about it, give you glowing testimonials—and still not use it regularly. And if they're not using it, they're not getting value, and they're certainly not paying for it. Consider how these relate to your own experience as a consumer. Think about all the apps on your phone that you thought were cool when you downloaded them. How many do you actually use daily or weekly? That's the gap between love and retention.

Getting There

There are three core tenets you should care about in the PMF universe.

First is *problem-solution fit*.
Have you built something people actually want and need?
Does it solve a real problem?
Are you looking at customer interviews, surveys, feedback? Are you measuring early-adoption rates and trying to quantify how painful the problem really is?

Next is *product-user fit*.
Do people love using your product?
Does it meet their needs and foster loyalty?
Are you able to see the "wow" moment for your customers?
Are you diving deep into user interviews, net promoter scores, retention rates, and engagement metrics?

Last is *business-market fit*.
Is your revenue model viable and scalable?
Can you monetize effectively?
Are you running pricing experiments; measuring willingness to pay; and tracking revenue growth, customer acquisition costs, lifetime value, churn rates, and profit margins?

We've already spent a good bit of time on problem-solution fit and later we'll get to business-market fit, so let's take a closer look at product-user fit. True product-user fit isn't just about creating those "wow" moments. It's about becoming an indispensable part of your users' lives or workflows. It's about creating habits, not just good impressions. It's about being the app they open first thing in the morning or the tool they can't imagine doing their job without.

Here's a tough question you need to ask yourself: If your product disappeared tomorrow, how many of your users would be genuinely upset? How many would scramble to find an alternative? That's the level of indispensability you're aiming for.

One of your challenges is to figure out how you can make your product so deeply integrated into your users' lives or workflows that the thought of switching to a competitor is truly painful. That's the kind of product-user fit that lasts. That's what turns users into evangelists and startups into unicorns. And that, my friend, is the target you should be aiming for.

Observability: I'm So Sorry to Do This to You Right Now

Get ready to meet your new best friend, whom you kinda hate, on this journey: *observability*. At its core, observability is just about keeping your finger on the (true) pulse of your product and your users.

I know what you're thinking. You have no real product, hardly any users, nothing. How the fuck can data be so important right now? And you're right. At the start, all you're going to have is gut feeling. But the sooner you start thinking about observability, the better off you'll be. This habitual way of thinking will push you to *always* ask, "How am I going to measure this? How will I know what's working?" You've heard it before, and you'll hear it again: You really can't manage what you can't measure. Observability, your superpower to see WTF is happening at a base level, involves tracking critical indicators.

Measure, Make Sense, and Take Action

Just as you can't manage what you can't measure, you can't improve what you can't see. Welcome to the world of observability, where real data meets gut feelings. Best-case scenario, observability supercharges your team with actionable insights.

Observability is more than collecting data. Deployed thoughtfully, it gives you the most valuable perspective of all, seeing your product through your users' eyes. This is the vantage point that helps you build a product that works the way your users want it to. It starts by understanding how they *actually* use it, not how you think they should use it.

Observability is the shortest route to answering a very, very reasonable question, in fact, the one question you most need to know: What's happening inside your application?

Your observability stack should cover three key areas:

1. The user: Track their every move, from demographics to in-app behavior.

2. The app: Monitor performance, errors, and feature usage.

3. The metal: Keep your servers and systems running smoothly.

This three-pronged approach allows you to connect dots that might otherwise remain unnoticed. For example, you may see a high volume of cart "abandons" and assume it's a pricing issue. But your observability stack might reveal that it's actually server latency causing users to give up. Only comprehensive data can help you uncover the real culprit.

What to Measure

Start with your North Star metric, the OMTM (Only Metric That Matters). The one metric you already defined that best captures the core value your product delivers to customers. Then, build out from there.

User journey: Follow what happens at each point, from first touch to conversion and beyond. Where do users drop off? Where do they get stuck?

Feature usage: Which features are being used? Which are ignored? Use this to guide product development priorities.

Performance metrics: Load times, error rates, application programming interface (API) response times—these technical metrics have a direct impact on user experience.

Retention and churn: Who stays? Who leaves? And most importantly, why?

User feedback: Both explicit (surveys, support tickets) and implicit (behavior patterns, usage data).

Sensemaking

Data without insight is just noise. Applying these best practices will turn that noise into understanding. First, look for patterns. Are there common characteristics among your power users? Among those who churn? Next, identify any friction points by tracking where users consistently struggle or drop off. Always, test your hypotheses. Use A/B testing to validate your assumptions about what will improve user experience or conversion rates. Not all users are created equal. How do different user groups interact with your product differently? Segment them. Finally, correlate metrics. How do changes in one area (e.g., load time) affect other areas (e.g., conversion rate)?

Data without insight **is just noise.**

Housekeeping Chores

Since it feels like you might actually be about to do this for reals, time to tackle some tangible bits. Let's take care of some functional, foundational stuff. The goal is to have something in place quickly so you can focus on building your minimum viable offering (MVO) and talking to potential customers. You can always refine and improve these elements as you go.

Secure your digital real estate. Register your domain name. Aim for a .com if possible. While you're at it, grab the same handle across major social media platforms (Twitter, LinkedIn, Instagram, etc.). If your exact name isn't available, consider adding "get" or "try" at the beginning. Consistency across platforms makes life easier for all.

Design logo version 1. Don't overthink. Spend $30 on a random freelancer to get a logo designed. We can change it every day, forever.

Set up a simple web presence. Use a template to build a basic "coming soon" landing page. Include a brief description of what you're building and an email sign-up form to capture interest. It's nothing to stress over or overspend, just a home address on the internet for now.

Set up a professional email. Create an email address with your domain name. It looks more professional than a generic carryover like jimmycollege18@gmail.com.

These steps serve multiple purposes. They make your startup feel more real, both to you and to anyone on the outside. They also protect your brand by ensuring no one else can grab your desired name or handles. Most importantly, they give you a home base, somewhere to start to build buzz around your idea.

Act on Insights

Observability isn't worth anything if the data doesn't drive action in key areas. Don't just notice something. Do something about it.

Prioritize development. Let usage data guide your product road map. Focus on improving the features that boost retention and conversion.

Personalize experiences. Use behavioral data to tailor the product experience for different user segments.

Problem-solve proactively. Set up alerts for unusual patterns so you can address issues before they become widespread problems.

Enhance marketing. Use insights about your most successful users to refine your target audience and messaging.

Improve continuously. Regularly review your metrics and set concrete goals for improvement.

Does Observability Really Matter?

Here's a "you can't make this stuff up" real-world example.

You're launching a new email service but oddly, people from Scunthorpe, UK, can't sign up because your system flags their city name as "offensive." How would you even know this is happening? That's a real question.

This wasn't some small startup. It was Gmail. Scunthorpe residents trying to create accounts were getting blocked and the process just... stopped. No explanation, no error message, just a dead end. All because Google's "offensive word filter" contained a certain four-letter word that happens to be inside "Scunthorpe."

This is why observability isn't afterthought—it's your lifeline. Without proper data analysis and monitoring, you'd never catch this kind of thing. Your eager potential Scunthorpe users would just disappear. Poof. Gone with no trace and no explanation.

Quirks like this demand that you obsess over identifying potential unintended consequences. They're the silent killers of startups. You need systems in place that signal when things go wrong in ways you never anticipated. Because they will. Keep asking, "What aren't we seeing? What could be happening that we don't know about?" The users who silently disappear are the ones you should be most worried about. They never get the chance to tell you why they left, and you never get the chance to welcome them back. What you don't know can and will absolutely fucking kill you.

Make It a Religion

Observability makes you challenge your assumptions. Then the data validates them or destroys them. It is not a set-it-and-forget-it tool. It's a mindset, a continuous process of measuring, learning, and improving. It's a tool to inform your decisions, not make them for you (just to make things even harder, sometimes the best product decisions are made against the data, based on a gut feeling).

You're constantly striving to close the gap between what you think your users want and what they actually need. Observability enables you to make informed decisions, iterate quickly, and build something truly exceptional. If you practice this from the beginning, by the time you have real users and real data, you'll have developed the habit of looking at your product with an analytical, unbiased eye. It's not easy, but if you do this you will guaranteed to be a thousand times ahead of others whose eyes are closed.

So before you ship, make sure you can observe. Make sure you can measure. Be committed to taking action. In the end, your ability to understand and act on user behavior will be the difference between a product that just works and a product that wins big.

The PMF Curse

When you hit real PMF, you'll know it. It's the intersectional moment when the market is desperate to buy (exchange value) what you're selling and users are persistent (rabid) in their usage. The transition to capturing that increased market share at velocity defines PMF. Your urgent job (not your only job!) pivots to recruiting. You're just trying to keep up. If you're not feeling that, you're not there yet.

Your business pre-PMF and post-PMF are two different companies. Pre-PMF, you are scrambling. You are doing everything; the whole house is on fire, always; it's literal mayhem. Everyone is wearing a million hats, doing whatever it takes, however it needs to happen. When PMF hits, suddenly you are operationalizing. It's the awful moment when you realize the competencies and team that got you *here* aren't the team to take you *there*. It's a brutal but necessary realization that we'll circle back to later.

Remember, you can create what you think is new in a garage, but the market defines if it's genuine innovation. The market is the ultimate judge of your product's value and relevance. Your opinion, my opinion, your mom's opinion—none of it matters compared to what the market thinks. Your market is customers who need/want/really must have *x* problem solved. Big companies are rarely desperate for anything, so don't begin by chasing them. That huge customer you think you want is likely not the actual customer you can have. Focus on the (probably much smaller) customers who feel an urgent need. These are the ones you can more realistically acquire early on.

So don't put "find PMF" on your founder's to-do list. Get out there and build something worth talking about. Then keep building, listening, measuring, improving. That's the real secret to product-market fit. It's about earning it every single fucking day. Build something so good, so in tune with your customers' needs, that PMF has no choice but to find you.

EARN IT: WHAT TO WATCH

Start building your observability mindset now, even before you have users. Think about what metrics would be most meaningful for your product. How will you track them? How often will you review them? Imagine what a sorry, missed opportunity it is to launch and not know where people get stuck, or bounce.

7

EARN THE RIGHT
TO BUILD SOMETHING

IF YOU'VE gotten this far, you've validated your problem and you've got a handle on your market. You're feeling ready, hopefully more ready than you've ever been. And that usually means you're itching to build your solution *now* and figure it all out later. A productive way to scratch that itch to *do* something is to take care of some basics. Now is a good time for some important housekeeping.

Feel better? Good, because I cannot scream this concept any louder, but I'll try.

DON'T BUILD YET.

Iterations done in your mind are free. Iterations with your (paid) engineer are costly. The playbook I'm coaching from is based on convincing you to iterate in your head so by the time you actually build, you know a touch more and are a touch more likely to create the *right* thing the first time.

Trust me, I've seen it a thousand times. First-time founders start building too early, convinced they have it completely mapped in their head. Halfway into the build they start seeing it come to life and it's not all that. Suddenly, they're adding features, piling on functions, or throwing in things they think the market absolutely must have, as if more features equate to additional customers or greater revenue. The product gets delayed. Costs pile up. Frantically, they're stacking shit on top of shit. By the time they're ready to go live, they know deep down that what they've built is seriously wrong. With what they now know, they're "ready" to build "for real" all over again, but they're out of money, out of time, and their credibility is not what it once was.

Don't Be That Founder

Before you dive into coding or prototyping or your Upwork engineer search, we need to talk about what it takes to earn the right to build something. Notice I said "build something," not "build your solution." Because we're still not 100 percent sold that your solution is the right solution. You've validated a problem, but the solution? That's still very much a work in progress whether you know it or not.

The solution in your head is probably right but very possibly also wrong. Or at least not as right as you think it is. There's a great quote often misattributed to Henry Ford: "If I asked people what they wanted, they would have said faster horses." In reality, what people probably wanted was to go faster. That means there were lots of potential solutions: lighter carriages, more horses, jet engines... cars! Your job isn't to build what people say they want. It's to solve their problem in a way that actually works, even if it's not what anyone expected.

There's a massive distinction here between the two crucial ways of defining your solution. You need to nail both aspects:

the *functional* jobs to be done and the *visionary* value delivery. Here's what I mean.

"Jobs to be done" is the nuts and bolts of what your solution actually does. It's the immediate, tangible function. The job of a hammer is to hit a nail. That's its function, plain and simple. What does your solution do? Maybe your app schedules meetings or your software analyzes data or your device measures something that needs extreme accuracy. Whatever it is, this is the basic *utility* of your product, and you should be able to clearly state this.

"Value delivery" is the bigger picture, the transformative impact your solution brings about. It's not what your product does but what it enables. The hammer's job is to hit nails, but its value delivery is in building homes or crafting furniture or creating art. It's about the change in the result. Can you define the broader impact your startup delivers? If your app schedules meetings, is its real value in reducing workplace stress, improving collaboration, driving better client outcomes, or increasing thinking time, for example?

Founder, before you build a single thing, your challenge is to honestly determine what solution will function well at its basic job but also deliver *transformative* value. That requires more than a tweak or a clever feature grafted onto any existing product. Too many founders focus solely on function and forget about value. Or they get lost in grand visions of value without nailing the basic functionality. It's not an either-or; it's really tough to pull off both.

Your users will come for the function, but they'll stay (and pay) only for the value. They'll download your meeting scheduler because they need to schedule meetings. But they'll become loyal paying customers because your solution has transformed their work life, reduced their stress, made them more productive, made life easier, and so on.

Calendly just books meetings. That's the job to be done. But its value delivery? Eliminating the awful back-and-forth of scheduling, saving hundreds of emails, and giving back hours of users' lives. That's why it's indispensable. Come for the function; stay for the impact.

Before you take each step forward, ask yourself, "What's the basic job my solution needs to do? What's the bigger value it's delivering? How can I make sure I'm nailing both?"

Full disclosure here, and I probably should have led with this confession: This chapter isn't about actually *building* your product. It's about figuring out what the hell you should be building in the first place. It's pushing you to relentlessly challenge your assumptions, test your ideas, and make sure you're not about to waste months building something nobody wants, even when it's a problem everyone wants solved. Earn the right to build something people want to pay for.

Something else to ponder at this point in your journey: "Pay" doesn't always mean cash. Payment comes in many currencies. Understanding this and expanding your definition of payment is crucial to your success. For some products, like Facebook, users pay with their time and attention—every minute spent scrolling is a form of payment. For others it might be data, personal information, or even reputation. Some B2B solutions might be paid for in equity or partnerships. And yes, sometimes it's cash. The key is to understand what form of payment your solution is asking for and then ensure that the value you're delivering is worth that price. Are you delivering enough value for users to pay with their time? Their data? Their cash? Remember, in the attention economy, a user's engagement can be as valuable as their credit card. Your job is to create something so valuable that users are willing to pay, in whatever form that payment takes.

What gets traction is an equitable transfer of value. If you're not delivering more value than you're asking in return, how can you possibly believe you will win?

Outcome-Driven Design: Find Your One Job

You're convinced you've got a killer product. But how can we check that feeling deep in your gut/head/heart? An effective place to start is using outcome-driven design (yeah, it's ODD). This isn't bullshit: Answering a few relevant questions about your solution (that still doesn't exist) helps determine if you're planning to build something people actually want and will use.

Your success in the market isn't determined by the complexity of your technology but by the simplicity and impact of the outcomes you deliver. You have to relentlessly focus on creating solutions that may be technologically complex and sophisticated under the hood but present themselves to users as elegant and simple tools that solve a problem effortlessly. Mastering the art of "sophisticated simplicity" means solving complex problems through solutions that feel intuitive and straightforward to your user. Users don't fall in love with your tech stack or how hard the problem was to solve or your sleepless nights or even the insane innovation you crafted under the hood. They fall in love with the way your product makes their lives easier or better.

Start with the loaded million-dollar question: What's the one thing your product absolutely has to do? I'm not talking about features or tech specs. I'm talking about outcomes. What's the one *metric* that moves significantly if your product is successful? This is your North Star, your OMTM.

Everything else is noise. If you can't define this, you're not ready to build anything. Full stop.

Consider Uber. What's their one job? Getting people from point A to point B quickly and reliably. That's it. Not the fancy app, not the surge pricing, not the ability to see your driver's face. Those are all features that support the core job. But the OMTM? It's probably something like "time from ride request to destination arrival." If it doesn't save you time, why would you use it?

Okay, I can already hear your pushback. "My product does so many things! It's revolutionary! It's going to change the world!" Slow your roll. I'm not questioning that your product will do many things or have multiple features. I'm saying that there's one core thing it needs to do and do it exceptionally well. There has to be *one* outcome it delivers that will make users say, "Holy shit, I need this in my life." That's the "transaction completion" step. Your thing did what it promised. High five.

You can apply the ODD process to your startup by working your way through this set of prompts (as always, it's only worth doing if you're honest, thoughtful, and not rushing to fill in the blanks).

List *all* the potential outcomes your product could deliver. Don't hold back. Go wild.

1. For each outcome, ask, "So what?" Keep asking until you hit bedrock—the fundamental value. This is crucial. You need to get to the root of why anyone (other than you) would give a damn about your product.

2. Prioritize these outcomes. Which one, if achieved, would make the others seem irrelevant or of less value?

Remember, users don't fall in love with features. **They fall in love with outcomes.**

3. Define how you'll measure this outcome. Be specific and quantifiable. If you can't measure it, you can't improve it. And if you can't measure it, your users can't either.

4. Validate this metric with potential users. Does it resonate with them? Do they give a shit about this outcome?

Again, Uber is a useful example.
Potential outcomes: Get a ride, save time, avoid parking hassles, reduce drunk driving, and so on.

1. "So what?" analysis:

    Get a ride > Save time > Do more important things > Improve quality of life

    Avoid parking > Reduce stress > Improve mood > Enhance overall well-being

    Reduce drunk driving > Save lives > Create safer communities

2. Prioritized outcome: Get from A to B safely and efficiently

3. OMTM: Time from ride request to destination arrival

4. Validation: Does this metric matter to users? (Erm... It does.)

Your OMTM becomes your North Star, guiding every decision. If a feature doesn't move this metric, it's a distraction. Period. This sounds harsh, but it's necessary. You have limited resources: time, money, energy. You can't afford to waste them on shit that doesn't matter.

This doesn't mean you ignore everything else. It means you prioritize ruthlessly. You focus on delivering that core value better than anyone else. Once you've nailed that, then you can start adding bells and whistles.

Remember, users don't fall in love with features. They fall in love with outcomes. They fall in love with the way your product makes their lives better. Focus on that, and you're already way ahead of 90 percent of the startups out there.

Minimum Viable Offering:
Less Than You Think, More Than You Hope

Alright, you're crystal clear on your OMTM. It's time to do it, figure out what you're actually going to build. You think it's the minimum viable product (MVP) you've heard about. MVP is real and true and all that, but even though no one asked for it, I'm giving you a new acronym with an important difference: minimum viable offering (MVO). The MVO asks you to build *less*. And if you haven't figured it out yet, that's what the ETR framework is all about: investing in doing the essential and avoiding the unnecessary.

"MVP, MVO, what's the difference?" I hear you ask. It's not just semantics. An MVP is often misunderstood as a half-assed version of your final product. That's not what we're after. An MVO is the *smallest thing* you can offer that delivers your OMTM. Nothing half-assed about it.

I want to double down on what this doesn't mean. It doesn't mean a shitty app. It doesn't mean a poor user experience. And it doesn't use the excuse "Oh, users know it's an MVP/beta." The market has moved. Given the lower cost and commodification of coding today, the first thing you release must let users achieve their outcome in a way that is at least moderately pleasing. Realistically, today's users expect a certain level of polish, even from new products. Your job is to find the sweet spot between "good enough to use" and "perfect but never shipped."

Design your MVO with a focus on outcomes, not features. Your MVO has to deliver that one core value proposition you identified.

Back to Uber again. Their MVO wasn't an app. It was a text message service that connected riders with drivers. That's it. No fancy user interface (UI), no ratings, no surge pricing. Just the core value proposition: Get from A to B. And it worked.

You've been thinking your solution has to be fully built out and complex. Remember, complexity is the enemy of execution. The more moving parts you have, the more things can go wrong. You can't possibly believe that your idea is more complex than Uber. So how did Uber make their idea seem so simple? They started with a clear OMTM and a basic model, then evolved over time to reach their current complexity, guided by user feedback and market opportunities.

This is a crucial point. Success often looks simple in hindsight. Don't let that fool you into thinking you need to build the entire vision right out of the gate. Your job is to find your starting point, your text-message-equivalent that solves the core problem. To identify your MVO, strip away everything that isn't absolutely essential to delivering your OMTM. Be ruthless. Be brutal. If it doesn't *directly* contribute to achieving your one job, no matter how clever or dazzling it is, it simply does not belong in your MVO.

This isn't about building a crappy product. It's focus. It's getting to market faster because you're not wasting time on irrelevant crap. It's learning what your users actually want, not what you think they want. Your users don't care about your vision for a perfect product. They care about solving their problem. If you can solve their problem with a text message service instead of a fancy app, do that. You can always add complexity later. But if you start complex and you're wrong about what users want, you've just wasted a ton of time and money.

Still need convincing? How about Dropbox. Their MVO wasn't even a working product. It was a simple explainer video that showed how the product would work. Their video generated a waiting list of 75,000 people. Only then did they start building the actual product. Why? Because they validated that people wanted the solution before writing a single line of code.

Nice, right? To launch with a waiting list of 75,000 hungry customers.

Repeat after me: "My MVO has to focus on outcomes, not features." What's the Only Metric That Matters to your users? What's the simplest possible way to deliver that outcome? Don't think about scalability. Don't think about your five-year vision. Think about solving the problem for one user, right now. If your OMTM is "reduce time spent on data entry," your MVO might be a simple form that autofills common fields. It's not sexy. It's not revolutionary. But if it solves the problem, if it moves the needle on the OMTM, it's enough to start with.

Your MVO is *not* your final product. It's a learning tool and a way to start delivering value while getting feedback as quickly (and inexpensively) as possible. You will iterate. You will improve. But you need to start somewhere, and that somewhere should be as simple as humanly possible without being half-assed. There is a difference and your users know it.

You're wondering about giving up competitive advantage, aren't you? Worrying someone will steal your idea if it's so simple. Ideas are worthless. Everybody has them. Execution is everything. Your competitive advantage isn't in some secret sauce or patented technology. It's in your ability to understand your users, learn quickly, and iterate faster than anyone else. (Sound familiar? That's your clock speed.)

If you are unable to defend against competition with a simple product, surely you won't be able to defend against it with a complex one. Your winning edge comes from your deep understanding of the problem and your relentless focus on solving it better than anyone else. Amazon started by selling only books. Facebook was a fun thing for college students. Google was just a search engine. They didn't try to boil the ocean from day one. They found their niche, dominated it, and then expanded. So annoyingly simple in hindsight. That's what you need to do: Find the annoyingly simple.

One final point: Don't mistake "simple" for basic or unimaginative. Each of these companies (Amazon, Facebook, Google) did something incredibly innovative within their narrow focus. Amazon wasn't just a bookstore; it was revolutionizing how people bought books, offering a selection no physical store could ever match. Facebook wasn't just another social network; it was creating a digital version of the college experience, starting with a closed, exclusive community. Google wasn't just another search engine; it was completely redefining how search results were ranked and presented. The genius of these companies wasn't in trying to do everything at once. Their success built on identifying *one core problem* they could solve better than anyone else, then executing based on that solution flawlessly. They were "simple" in their initial focus but not in their innovation or ambition.

One more final point: Be uncompromising in your efforts to be audaciously good at solving one specific problem. Your MVO should be simple in its scope but revolutionary in its execution. It should make people say, "Why didn't I think of that?" or "How did we ever live without this?" That's the kind of simple you're aiming for. The kind that makes success look inevitable. In hindsight, disruption often looks obvious. Can you find that obvious-in-hindsight solution that nobody's executed well yet? That's your beachhead. That's your MVO. That's how you earn the right to build an empire. Focus on doing one thing exceptionally well. Solve one problem better than anyone else. Exhale. We're not done getting you ready to build yet, but let's change the pace.

Prototyping: Fake It 'til You Make It (Not)

Prototyping is another term that comes with tons of baggage, most of it misguided. The goal of a prototype is not to build your product (although sometimes it is). You prototype to learn about your product. This is where reality kicks in, where your idea starts to take shape. You want to move your solution as far down the track as humanly possible *before* you write a line of code. Prototyping spurs you to answer many questions, think through scenarios, fight for simplicity, and, most of all, sit in the customer's seat for the first time.

Prototyping can tackle different unknowns. Perhaps you need to prove that something is technically feasible. Maybe you want to explore user interaction. Maybe you want a rough version of your actual solution. The key is using prototyping as a learning and iteration tool, not a final product.

Different forms of prototypes are useful at different stages of solution development. Here are some options for you to consider before you start the process.

Paper prototypes: Actual paper (or paper alternatives). Sketches. Diagrams. Flowcharts. Rapid ideations. Start testing and mapping out basic concepts and user flows without investing in a single line of code. Don't underestimate the power of this. Almost all founders start with some sort of sketch, sometimes even on the legendary cocktail napkin.

Clickable mock-ups: Tools like Figma let you create interactive designs without coding. This is great for testing user interfaces and basic functionality. You can create something that looks and feels like a real app, without the overhead of actual development.

Wizard of Oz prototypes: This is where it gets fun. You fake the tech but deliver the service manually. Zappos started this way: They didn't build a complex inventory system, they just went to shoe stores and bought the shoes people ordered. It's labor-intensive, but it lets you test your value proposition without building anything.

Concierge MVP: Similar to Wizard of Oz, but even more hands-on. You deliver your core value proposition as a high-touch service to a small number of users. This lets you learn exactly what users value before you build anything automated.

Actual mini build: Sometimes your prototype might be a stripped-down version of your actual product. This could be a basic web app, a simple mobile app, or even a physical product. It's functional enough to test your core value proposition but not so complex that it takes months to build.

Choose the prototype that lets you learn the most with the least build-out cost and effort. The sweet spot you're searching for exists between realism and speed of development. I'll say it again: Do not build anything you don't absolutely need to validate your core assumptions.

One way to get the most from your prototype is to put yourself in the user's seat. Go screen by screen, page by page, function by function. Start at the beginning: A user logs in, and now what, now what, now what, now what. Why? Why? Why? Why? If you are paying attention as you follow the user journey, there is no scenario on earth under which you don't see an opportunity, an adjustment, an iteration. You are actually building out a view through the user's eyes, and damn, that is eye-opening (welcome to empathy).

Done right, this process will lead to a boatload of information coming at you. Here are two ways to simulate user experience:

1. Flowchart: Scrutinize all the steps, all the decision trees, every screen from when the user arrives on the website landing page to when the user completes the transaction. *Say everything out loud.*

This process, formally known as "rubber duck debugging," is the same thing I urged you to do before. Yes, it sounds ridiculous, but it's a game-changer. Trust me. Get a rubber duck (or any inanimate object), put it on your desk, and explain your entire user journey to it. Out loud. Start from the moment a user lands on your website and narrate *every single step* until they complete a transaction.

Don't skip anything. Visualize it. Don't use vague terms like "thing" or "bit" or "they click a button." What button? What exactly happens when they click it? If they're signing up, what fields are they filling out? Why those specific fields? Again and again, after every step, the duck asks, "Why?"

This process forces you to articulate every minute detail you might otherwise gloss over in your head. Why do we need a phone number? Why do we even need a name? All the way into the more functional "How do we actually transition to the next page?" For each step, the duck wants to know "What's the point? What's the objective?" What *you* want to know to spare your user pain is "What can we remove?" Guaranteed, you'll uncover gaps in your logic, unnecessary steps, and friction points you hadn't considered. You might realize you're asking users to make five clicks when one would do or that you're requesting information you don't actually need but think you do because so many other websites ask for it.

This exercise isn't just about refining your solution. It helps you truly understand every detail of your user's experience. Plus, you get the fab experience of feeling like a lunatic talking to a rubber duck for an hour.

What's obvious to you isn't obvious to your users. It's fresh eyes (and a rubber duck) catching those "oh, shit" moments before your users do. Detailed realizations like these can make the difference between a clunky product and one that feels effortlessly intuitive. It's also the first big step to user empathy!

2. Wireframes: Using any tool, you should build what it could look like—not design, only function. This helps you visualize the user interface and interaction points without getting into visual design.

Both of these methods force cost-free iterations, give insights into easier ways to accomplish tasks, reveal what data we really need, and help us assess what actually has to happen at various points. They strip your ideas down to essentials, giving you a better understanding of what's crucial for delivering value to your users.

Personally, I'm a Balsamiq user. It's the lowest-lift, highest-value tool for me to convert my ideas into a visual format without a steep learning curve. My practice is to have every screen and every flow mapped out. The massive win (pretty much every time) is that you will bounce into a better idea, a better way, a breakthrough.

The power of prototyping is not building fast; it's fast learning. Providing your service manually in an unscalable, awful way. Actually doing it without the technology. So much cheaper to make your mistakes on paper (or in a simple mock-up) than in code. Get feedback early and often, then use it when you start building for real. You'll have gained much deeper insight into what you are going to build and how it's going to work for your user.

Like most of the other work I've urged you to invest in so far, prototyping is for *you*, to understand, iterate, develop. Your prototype doesn't need to be pretty or polished. It needs to be functional enough to test your assumptions and get meaningful feedback. Rough prototypes can sometimes be better: They encourage users to focus on functionality rather than getting hung up on design. Use prototyping to experiment, try wild ideas, fail cheaply, and learn quickly. Embrace it. Maybe even have fun with it.

I know this feels like a monstrous amount of work that doesn't add up to actual product development. But trust me here, smart prototyping will save you *months* of building the wrong thing. Better yet, it will save you from the soul-crushing experience of launching a product nobody wants.

Smoke Signals

Now for a concept that may be new to you and possibly sound intriguing, even cool. It's the ultimate reality check: the smoke test. Here's where your assumptions collide with reality, and you learn more about your product and market in a few days than you have in months of planning (and praying).

Why run a smoke test? It's a rapid, low-cost experiment designed to validate your core assumptions before you invest heavily in building your product. Real-world feedback, fast. If you cannot prove that what you're offering is of value, then nothing else, and I mean absolutely nothing else, matters.

Reasons to run a smoke test:

It's cheap: It's way cheaper than building a full product only to find out no one wants it.

It's fast: You can run a smoke test in days, not months.

It's real: You're dealing with actual potential customers, not hypotheticals or avatars.

What might a smoke test look like? Say you have an idea, a core thesis, and maybe one image or some text that you think is a decent hook. You create a landing page using any number of free templates, build an ad based on the core pain your users have, and then see how many clicks the ad gets or how many people enter their email to "learn more." Surely that's a tell.

You can run this play in a million ways. Now that you know what a smoke test is, you've probably encountered some software sign-ups that mysteriously errored out, for instance. That was probably a smoke test, looking to see if they could get you to sign up.

The smoke test can take many forms with the goal of colliding with reality in some manner to measure something, somehow. Maybe it's to have a front so you can speak to prospects or angels. There are plenty of incredible websites that look and feel like real products, but they're just testing the market. I hear the rumblings of Theranos. Smoke testing is for legitimate learning and assumption validation. Fraud is deceiving for personal gain. It's crucial to understand the difference.

Your smoke test is not designed to trick or take advantage of people. You sincerely want to learn if there's genuine interest in your solution. You're not selling snake oil; you're investigating to determine if there's a market for the very real thing you want to offer.

Once you've run your initial smoke test you enter a loop of constant experimentation.

Step 1: Deploy. Get your test out there.
Step 2: Measure. Collect data obsessively.
Step 3: Learn. Analyze what the data is telling you.
Step 4: Iterate. Make changes based on what you've learned.
Step 5: Repeat: Do it all over again.

Recognize that motion? Yup, that's clock speed in action. Run experiments on anything and everything. Your pricing, your messaging, your features, your target market. Each experiment brings you closer to the truth of what your market actually wants.

Just sayin', your first smoke test will probably fail. Maybe the second and third will too. But each "failure" is actually a success because you're learning. You're getting closer to product-market fit (PMF again) without blowing your entire budget.

Remember, at this stage, speed is your friend. Don't spend weeks debating the perfect test. Run it. Learn from it. Move on. Your goal is to fail fast, learn fast, and improve fast, *all before you build*. This process is less about validating your product and more about training you, the founder, to be responsive to market feedback. It is the CEO muscle-building workout of listening to your users and iterating quickly, strengths that will keep on serving you long after you've launched your product.

Resource Allocation: Spend Wisely, Learn Fast

Points to you. You've been patient getting through all this when what you really want to do is hire developers and start coding. Writing that first line of code feels like progress, like you're finally doing something real. But hurry slowly. The build phase is where most startups hemorrhage cash with little to show for it. Almost everything I've asked you to do up until now has been free(ish). Costing you time but not money. Now you have to come to terms with what resources you have, where you are in the process, and how well you are able to execute. Code is cheap but expensive in context. Every line of code you write is a line you'll have to maintain, debug, and potentially rewrite. And if you're building the wrong thing, all that code becomes really expensive waste.

How do you allocate your resources wisely? Here's my advice.

Prioritize learning over building. Spend money on customer interviews, prototypes, and tests before you spend a dime on development. Yes, it feels less tangible. But the insights you gain will be worth their weight in gold.

Use no-code tools where possible. You'd be surprised how much you can do without custom code. Tools like Zapier, Airtable, and Webflow can take you further than you might think. Don't be too proud to use them. If you simply must code, start with a functional backend and a bare-bones frontend. Pretty UIs are for later. Focus on making it work before you make it look good.

Outsource wisely. Don't offshore your core competency, but don't waste time reinventing wheels either. Use APIs and third-party services for non-core functionalities.

Set clear milestones. These should be tied to learning objectives, not development goals. "Implement user authentication" is not a good milestone. "Validate that users are willing to create an account to use our service" is.

Remember, every dollar you spend should bring you closer to proving (or disproving) your core value proposition. If you can't draw a clear line between an expense and your OMTM, think twice about it. And think again. I once worked with a startup that blew through $500,000 building a beautiful app with all the bells and whistles. Know what happened? Nobody downloaded it. Why? Because they spent all their time and money building and no time understanding their users. They could have learned the same lessons with a $5,000 prototype and some customer interviews. Don't be a casualty of wishful thinking. Be smarter. Be leaner. Be open. Be focused on learning.

Thinking in terms of experiments, not features, is a powerful guide. Every bit of resources you allocate should be towards testing a hypothesis. "We believe that users will pay x dollars for y feature" is a hypothesis. Build the minimum thing required to test that. Nothing more.

And for fuck's sake, don't waste money on vanity. No, you don't need custom swag. You don't need a fancy office. You don't need to attend every conference under the sun. You need to solve a problem for your users. Full stop.

Runway is runway. Once it's gone, it's gone. Treat every dollar like it's your last, because it might be. The startups that survive aren't the ones with the most funding. They're the ones that learn the fastest and adapt the quickest. The ones truly in it, for the long haul, are frugal. The ones in it for the vanity have all the bits and, too often, only bits to show for it.

Did We Win? The Moment of Truth

You've defined your OMTM. You've created your MVO. You've prototyped and smoke-tested. You've allocated your resources wisely (hopefully). But have you actually earned the right to build? This is your moment of truth. This is where you look yourself in the mirror and answer honestly: Am I ready to bet everything on this?

Building a product is expensive and time-consuming. You owe it to yourself (and your future users) to be damn sure you're building the right thing. Because once you start building, the clock starts ticking. And in the land of startups, time is a resource you can never get back. Building is not the goal. The goal is to solve a problem. If you can solve the problem without building, do that. Your users don't care about your code. They care about the outcome you deliver.

You've earned the right to build when you're so confident in your solution that you're willing to bet everything on it. Because, let's face it, that's exactly what you're about to do.

Now What?

Building is just the beginning. Once you build, you enter a whole new world of challenges. User acquisition. Retention. Scaling. But those are problems for another day. For now, focus on building the right thing. Everything else follows from that.

Don't forget why you started this journey in the first place. It's easy to get lost in the weeds of product development, to get so focused on features and timelines that you lose sight of the bigger picture. But at the end of the day, you're not just building a product.

You're solving a problem. You're making someone's life better. Never lose sight of that.

Okay founder, you are on your way, and if you're still pumped to build, if you've done the work and you're ready to commit, then godspeed. You've earned it. Go forth and build something worth using. See you in the next chapter.

> ## EARN IT
>
> Are you really ready to put your idea to the test? To let the market tell you if you're on the right track? It's scary, I know. But it's a hell of a lot less scary than spending months or years building something nobody wants. Fire up that landing page. Craft that ad. Define your success metrics. And let your smoke test fly. The market is waiting to tell you what it thinks. Are you ready to listen?

8

EARN THE RIGHT TO DELIGHT

YOU'RE HERE to create an experience so good, so seamless, so completely *delightful* that your users can't help but come back for more and bring their friends. Life without your creation is simply unthinkable. Reactions this strong don't come from features or brilliant code or your fab UI. This emotional moment happens when a user first interacts with your product and thinks, "Holy shit. This is amazing."

That, my friend, is *experience*.

Building for user delight isn't some weirdo bullshit. It forms the cornerstone of your entire business. Seems bizarre, right? What the hell does emotion (experience) have to do with your SaaS solution or your B2B platform? You're solving a problem, not running a therapy session or creating art. I hear you asking, "How the fuck can my medical coding app evoke an emotional response from a healthcare professional?"

Well, it can because we humans are emotional creatures, even when we're using software. Maybe especially when we're using software.

When was the last time you talked about or shared an app that excited you? What made it amazing: the fifty-seven features or how it made you feel smart or productive or connected? Maybe it made your life easier in a surprising, delightful way. Experience goes deeper than making your app shoot confetti every time someone logs in (if you have to do that, please do it privately). A positive emotional response has to come from addressing things your user is dealing with: frustrations, aspirations, expectations. Your job is to create moments of relief, joy, or even triumph as they use your product.

Emotional connections like these turn casual users into die-hard fans, the folks who stick around even when bugs pop up or features are missing, the ones who forgive your mistakes and celebrate your successes. A "wow" user experience buys you time on everything you haven't done yet. One could say it's the basis for a sustainable business.

Design for Delight?

Aiming to design your solution as a direct line to an emotional feeling of triumph sounds crazy. Let's focus instead on how your solution engages, retains, delivers, and converts. It comes down to some inescapable metrics: Was your solution simple, was it easy, did it do the job, or did it make life measurably better?

This isn't just about making things pretty. Of course they should be. It's about engineering an experience from the ground up. Every click, every load time, every interaction, word, image, thing is a chance to win or lose a user. You're not just showcasing features. You're setting the expectations for your entire relationship with that user in the most epic fight of all: to keep them from leaving your site without getting to know (and love) your amazing product.

Every profession has its "jobs to be done," the necessary tasks or processes that cause some form of pain. We realize that coming into the market with a small, incremental improvement isn't enough. You need to create something that doesn't just solve a problem but does so in a way that makes users feel understood, empowered, and maybe even a little bit delighted. More and more, the solutions that look to take over the existing market dominators focus on experience. This chapter is about creating the experience that delivers the "Holy shit, this is amazing" response, even when your app is solving for functional, technical, non-emotive problems.

Do you deliver the 10x feature that makes you a compelling alternative to the market leader? Or is the experience "meh" or even less?

To get to "Holy shit," you're going to have to painstakingly cycle through multiple processes that can lead you to discover delight. I'm asking you to push through rounds of repetition, because each time you meticulously, hypercritically map out your user journey or evaluate your friction points, you are creating an opportunity. A chance to see something you missed before. Detect a crack in your assumptions. Catch a flash of insight. Arrive at a moment of brilliant realization ("How did I not see that before?") that changes *everything*.

Think of it like walking a loop trail clockwise, then doing it counterclockwise. You will absolutely see things you missed. The exercises in this chapter are *forced iterations* because you make discoveries only when you keep searching.

The Golden Rules of an ETR Golden Handshake

Picture your first encounter with a stranger. You probably smile, make eye contact, and reach out for a firm handshake. In these very brief moments, as few as eight seconds, a lot of information gets silently exchanged. And we all know you don't get a second chance at a first impression.

Your landing page is your first impression, the place where what I call the golden handshake has to happen. You have only precious seconds of time spent on clicks, steps, buttons before a user decides if your product is worth their time. Your job is to stop them from leaving.

Don't believe it? Google found that users form an opinion in *milliseconds*. Amazon Web Services reports that a poor experience turns away 88 percent of users. The Baymard Institute found better checkout design increases conversions by 35.26 percent. The data goes on and on and on. I didn't believe it, so I tested it on my newsletter. Initially, I asked for a first name and email. Data says removing the first name requirement will increase sign-ups by 15 percent. I eliminated the question. Sign-ups rose by 23 percent. Immediately. Really, why did I think I needed that first name? Just so I could start my newsletter with "Hey, Bob"?

Those initial eight seconds are brutal. If we think of the broad flow that has to happen from pre-hello through value delivery, there are several essential components that you have to break down, fast, each with their own objective and requirements.

Sourcing and first impressions: The make-or-break moment is your landing page. Is it clear and compelling? Does it immediately communicate value? Give the user what they need? Help them on their journey? Please do not make me dig to find what I need. If you want the user to sign up or contact you, what must you provide for the user to want to take that next step?

If you are forcing your users into a sales call just to get a demo or insisting they enter their email to download your ebook or hiding pricing behind some sales wall, you may think you're being clever, but you will never know how many users got annoyed and just left. Many founders complain, "If they could only see how amazing my product is," but you're the one driving them away needlessly.

Frictionless entry: Sign-up should be seamless. Every field you ask users to fill out is a potential exit point. Use auto options, progressive profiling, and smart defaults to make this process as fast and painless as possible. Don't gather one single iota more data than you need. Do the work *for* your users everywhere you can.

Orientation and contextualization: Once they're in, guide users where they need to be. Personalized onboarding is a mandate. Show users exactly how your product fits into their life or workflow.

First active engagement: This is *it*. The aha moment when they see the core value of your product. Get them there as quickly as possible.

Value realization: Show, don't tell. Provide immediate, tangible value. If your product is a productivity app, help users complete a task. If your product is an analytics tool, give them an instant insight. Think "test drive" or "live demo."

Next steps and continued value: The golden handshake doesn't end after eight seconds, not if you want to build a following. Set clear next steps, showcase future value, and give users a reason to come back.

Getting users in is 98 percent of the battle.

The Minimum Delightful Experience (MDE)

Although I mentioned it earlier, I don't actually believe in minimum viable product (MVP) anymore. Nobody wants "minimum viable," not even early adopters. What grabs them is the minimum *delightful* experience (MDE).

But the acronym is not important; what matters is what it represents. MDE is the smallest set of features and interactions that not only solves the user's problem but also creates a positive emotional response. You can hear the difference from the user who says, "Yeah, this works" or "Wow, this is awesome!" or (forgive me...) "Holy shit, this is amazing."

Building your MDE is an iterative process. I know, another one of those. Start by identifying what the "wow" moment is. What's the one interaction or result that will make users sit up and take notice? This is your North Star; it's what completes the transaction. Do everything in your power to accelerate and reduce friction on the way to "wow." The OMTM is how you *measure* the impact of your North Star.

That means stripping away all nonessentials. If a feature doesn't directly contribute to that "wow" moment or solve the core problem, it doesn't belong in your MDE. Be ruthless. Toss it. The path to "wow" should be smooth and intuitive. Every click, every screen, every interaction should feel purposeful and effortless, clearly signaling you are going somewhere worth getting to.

Along the user journey, add unexpected value. Are there small touches that can delight? Maybe it's a clever bit of microcopy, a thoughtful default setting, or a subtle animation that makes an action feel more satisfying. (Confetti throwing again? Probably not.) At essence, you must nail the basics. Ensure that your core functionality is rock-solid. A delightful experience built on a shaky foundation cannot last.

Your MDE isn't set in stone. It's a starting point, a hypothesis about what will resonate with your users. You'll iterate and expand it based on real user feedback and behavior. Start here and you're already miles ahead of the competition who thinks the battle is in technical competency and features, the ones who can't wait to drag the user through endless screens to show it all off.

Engineering Delight

Those are two words you don't often see paired. But delight is more than a feeling. It's a metric for your product impact, maybe even for your success that doesn't result from winging it. You need to engineer for it. The target is to hit the "Oh fuck" conversion metric indicating how quickly and how often a user thinks "oh fuck, that's good" as many times as possible in those first user-engagement moments.

How do you bake delight into your product?

Like any good gift, satisfaction starts by anticipating needs. Don't wait for users to ask for what they want. Predict what they'll need and provide it before they even realize they want it. A study by Salesforce found 62 percent of users expect you to anticipate their needs. Living up to that expectation is step one of delivering delight. Then build some above and beyond features, something they wouldn't expect but you

The first version of your product probably won't be as delightful as you hope. That's okay. **It's a journey to get closer to that ideal delightful experience.**

think they'll love. Maybe it's an extra layer of analysis in your reporting tool, something that's core but unexpected—that shows you truly understand your customer.

With thought and experimentation, you can design some cool micro-interactions. These may be small animations, transitions, and feedback mechanisms that make using your product feel good. A satisfying "swoosh" when completing a task, an encouraging message when hitting a milestone—these little touches add up. Mine the data you have to make each user's experience feel tailored to them. Address them by name, remember their preferences, suggest actions based on their behavior; in short, do whatever you can to personalize their interaction.

Delight is about showing users you understand them, value their time, and are committed to making their lives better. It's about creating an emotional connection that turns users into fans and fans into evangelists. In truth, evangelists are the foundation of almost any growth strategy.

The Friction Equation

For every moment of delight, there's a potential moment of frustration. Your job is to minimize these friction points and solve for the "friction equation":

user satisfaction = value delivered / user effort required

Yeah, you already know this, the crucial importance of maximizing value while minimizing effort. Still, it's amazing how many founders forget it. They pile on features, thinking more is better, when all they're really doing is increasing the user effort required. The trap every founder finds irresistible is adding "just one more thing" in the misguided belief that one more feature will make or break the product. Feature creep. Sometimes it's the result of valid learning and feedback, sure. But if it's not directly contributing to your North Star metric, it's a dangerous siren song that's damn near impossible to resist. It's noise-cancelling-headphones time, founders.

Staying relentlessly focused is one of the toughest challenges you'll face as a founder. Learning to say no to good ideas so you can say yes to great ones. Never backing away from urgently prioritizing what truly matters for your users. Distraction is also friction.

There's no way to do this right without feeling like you're spinning in circles. Auditing your user journey has to keep happening until you find the glide path. Map out—in a diagram, as a flowchart—every step a user takes, from first hearing about your product to becoming a power user. Where are the potential friction points?

Every extra click, every moment of confusion, every second of load time is a potential lost user. Simplify by cutting anything that doesn't directly contribute to value delivery. That includes making users think too much. Build in smart defaults based on user behavior and industry standards. No one appreciates being overwhelmed by an avalanche of options. Progressive disclosure reveals features and information as users need them.

Then there's error prevention. This is not bug prevention. It's designing the journey with guardrails to protect your user from mistakes. Constraints, clear labels, and an intelligent design guide users to success. And does it even need to be stated that lightning-fast load times are a necessity? Optimize your product relentlessly. Every millisecond counts.

In the natural world, we can never eliminate all friction, and frankly, friction isn't always bad. Sometimes, a moment of friction can enhance the overall experience by creating investment into your product, separating real users from the window-shoppers while adding superior quality. The key is to make sure any friction works for you by delivering more value than the effort it requires.

Data-Driven Delight

Please do not try implementing all these process improvements without committing to tracking every aspect of user interaction. Without measurement, you're flying blind. As the saying goes, you can't manage what you cannot measure. You can't see signals in things you don't track. Without data, you have no idea what the fuck is happening. You have to move off your gut to real information. With your tiny set of initial users, observability can be a conversation, a manual process that starts with your early adopters. What do you want to ask your first cohort of users? The obvious questions are, "Did it work?" and "Did it do what it said it would?" Over time, you'll get better at asking better questions. Think about the suggestions below as a way to shape questions that help you understand if you fulfilled your promise. You'll have a better understanding of the barriers to acquiring and retaining users.

Feel free to develop your own standards for delight, but here are some fundamentals to get you started.

- Time to value: How long does it take for a new user to experience the core value of your product?
- Task completion rate: What percentage of users successfully complete key tasks? Where are they dropping off? Why?

- User effort score: How much effort do users have to expend to accomplish their goals?

- Net promoter score: Would users recommend your product to others? This is a flawed but key indicator of overall satisfaction.

- Feature adoption rate: Which features are users actually using? Which are being ignored? Why?

- Retention rate: Are users coming back? How often? For how long?

- "Oh fuck" metric: How many moments of delight are users experiencing? You can measure this crazy but important metric through surveys, user testing, and analyzing user behavior around certain features.

You've got the data. Now you need a system for figuring out how this data can further your vision, your nuance, your understanding by fueling continuous improvement. Ongoing, constant refinement happens only when you commit to regular user testing, observing real users interacting with your product. Make it easy for users to provide feedback and have a feedback loop for quickly responding, and that includes support issues. Iterate rapidly (clock speed) to demonstrate through frequently shipped updates that you are responding and evolving.

Metrics are indicators, not definitive measures of delight. Use them as guides, pair them with qualitative insights and your own judgment. Numbers can tell you what's happening, but they can't always tell you why. That's what your gut is for.

The Full-Stack Experience

Founders often think user experience is just about the product. It's not. It's about every single touchpoint a user has with your company. Your marketing, your sales process, your customer support—it's all part of the experience. Your user's journey doesn't start when they log into your app. It starts the moment they hear about you from an ad, a recommendation, a Google search, or your content. Immediately, you're setting expectations you have to be ready to meet.

That means clear, consistent messaging across all channels. The value you propose with your product should match what users experience with your product. Anything less is a broken promise or, worse, a deception.

Users should be able to reach you however they want, via chat, email, phone, or some clear next steps you provide for them. And the experience should be consistently excellent across all channels.

Transparency rules. Keep your users in the loop to build trust, because trust is the foundation of all lasting relationships. Provide time reports, open road maps, honesty about problems. Users are so forgiving when you are up front. Users don't examine your organizational chart, and they sure don't care which team is responsible for which part of their experience. They just want things to work and work well. Every time.

There's a dark side to delight that is easy to succumb to. Things to avoid start with unnecessary animations, cutesy microcopy, or forced "personality" that can quickly go from delightful to annoying. Your users are trying to get shit done. Don't let your attempts at manufacturing faux delight get in their way.

Let's not create dark patterns: design tricks that manipulate users into doing things they didn't intend. They might boost your short-term metrics, but they create negative emotions. That's literally the opposite of what we're doing here.

User-centricity can't be a bolt-on or an afterthought. It needs to be the foundation of your entire company. Because in the end, your product isn't just what you're selling—it's the entire experience you're providing. Find the right balance. Delight should enhance the core experience, not detract from it. It should feel natural, unforced, genuine, and benevolent.

If it makes sense for your product, consider building a community as a potent source of support, ideas, and loyalty. Having an army of advocates who not only use your product but champion it and perhaps even help each other with their problems is incredibly powerful.

The ROI of Delight

I know how hard it is to convert delight into dollars and metrics into revenue. It might not always be the straightest line, but there is no way any of us would disagree that helping someone have a better day by doing a thing well can only be good. Here are some ways in which delight can be rewarding.

- Increased retention: Delighted users stick around. In the subscription economy, reducing churn is often more valuable than acquiring new users.
- Word-of-mouth marketing: Happy users become your best marketers. In a world of increasing ad costs, organic growth is gold.

- Reduced support costs: When your product is intuitive and delightful, users need less hand-holding. This means lower support costs for you.

- Premium pricing power: Users are willing to pay more for products they love. Delight can justify higher price points.

- Competitive advantage: In crowded markets, user experience can be your key differentiator.

- Increased lifetime value: Delighted users are more likely to upgrade, buy additional products, or expand their usage.

- Attracting talent: Great designers and engineers want to work on products that users love. A reputation for delight can help you attract top talent.

The bottom line? Delight isn't just a nice-to-have. It's a powerful business strategy that drives growth, retention, and profitability.

Shipping Delight

You've done the work. You've crafted your golden handshake, engineered moments of delight, ruthlessly eliminated friction, set up your data tracking. Now it's time to ship your vision to engineering.

Don't get caught in an endless cycle of tweaks and improvements, always finding one more thing to polish before launch. Don't.

Delight is subjective and contextual. You won't know for sure what delights your users until you get your product in their hands. So ship. Ship early, ship often... clock speed.

When you ship, ship with intention. Have clear hypotheses about what will delight users and how you'll measure it. Set up your analytics to track the metrics and have a plan. Surely, you are not building anything without an outcome in mind, which means surely, you can set a metric to determine if the change was successful.

The first version of your product probably won't be as delightful as you hope. That's okay. It's a journey to get closer to that ideal delightful experience.

The Never-Ending Quest

Here's the thing about delight: It's a moving target. What delights users today might be table stakes tomorrow. The bar for good experiences is constantly rising. This means your job is never done. You need to stay curious, stay hungry. Keep talking to your users. Keep experimenting. Keep pushing the boundaries of what's possible.

First-time founders, after you release, go into incognito mode, create a new email account, and go through your own app, step by step, slowly and with intention. There is no way you won't find something…

All this talk about delight seems like bullshit when you're at day zero. You don't have a product. You don't have investors. You don't have users. You've got nothing but an idea. But if we agree that getting users and driving growth is the goal and that real growth comes from users who stick around, then delight isn't just some concept. It's a gnarly competitive advantage, especially in a crowded market.

Just maybe every decision you make, every line of code you write, every pixel you push—it all needs to be in service of creating that delight. Because when you nail that, everything else falls into place.

How do you know when you've earned the right to delight? It's not just about metrics or user acquisition. It's about seeing your product take on a life of its own. You'll know you're on the right track when users start finding creative ways to use your product that you hadn't even considered. When they're pushing your product beyond its intended purpose because it's become indispensable to them. That's when.

So, let's create experiences that make users smile, that make their lives easier, that they can't help but share with others because you're not just building a product. You're crafting experiences. You're solving problems. You're making people's lives better, easier, more enjoyable. That's the power of delight.

If this is too much positivity for a startup founders book and you need to vent, feel free to go scream at some puppies.

EARN IT: FOUR NOT-SO-SIMPLE STEPS

1. Be a power user of your own product. Practice "dogfooding," which means using your own product extensively before expecting others to embrace it. If you (or those close to you) are not delighted by your product, how do you expect anyone else to be?

2. Study the masters. Look at products you love. What makes them delightful? Don't just imitate them—understand the principles behind their choices.

3. Cultivate empathy. Put yourself in your users' shoes. What are they feeling when they use your product? What do they need that they might not even be able to articulate?

4. Experiment constantly. Try new things. Not everything will work, but each experiment will teach you something.

9
EARN THE RIGHT TO SHIP

EVERYTHING, AND I MEAN every fucking thing, changes when actual humans start poking at your product. Not your mum, not your best friend, but a live, random human who found your product, believed your sales pitch, and chose to try it out.

This chapter won't hold your hand through the build process. It's not a step-by-step guide on how to code or find your first engineer. I'm not going to explain or advocate for methodologies like agile or waterfall. Instead, this chapter will arm you with the insights, tools, and mindset you need to *ship something that matters*. Something that delights. Something that has a shot at making a dent. Most importantly, this stage is about understanding your role as a founder in the build process and beyond.

It's Ship Time

Earning the right to ship is the real deal of turning that idea in your head into something tangible that users touch, use, love, or hate. Until you ship, you're not really in the arena. You're still just a spectator.

Ship time is the moment the market will see what you stand for, what you are capable of, whether you are the real deal. Because they're so fucking terrified of putting something imperfect out into the world, too many founders get lost in endless cycles of engineering more features, more tweaks, more adjustments. They burn through cash and never ship anything at all.

Steel yourself to build less. Actually less. The only perfect line of code is no line of code. Your idea gets into the marketplace only if you ruthlessly prioritize, kill everything that isn't a core deliverable of your solution, and never get distracted by green-lighting features that might be irresistibly incredible but don't serve your essential purpose.

To ship code means having real code written, run through a system to ensure it moderately works, then made "live" for someone to use. So when your engineer shows you a feature or thing that's ready and in testing, it's up to you and only you to go live and meet your audience. And it's done with two simple but courageous words: "Ship it!"

Why are you the one to make the call? Simple. Because if it breaks, it's on you. Not your engineer. You want to own that responsibility, because it will break. As the founder, you decide what bugs or embarrassment or unfinished elements you'll accept. You dictate whether it is ready to meet your audience—and how you will respond when the inevitable flaws appear.

Remember, you are not merely building a product. You're building a *solution* to a problem. Keep your eyes on the problem, not your code. The moment you fall in love with your solution more than the problem you're solving is the moment you start to fail, because you are looking at the business through an inverted lens: one that magnifies the beauty of your solution and diminishes the dimensions of the problem.

Everything you've done up to this moment has been hard. But going public, actually walking into the arena, is even harder. You might be feeling like an impostor right now. Good. That means you're pushing yourself out of your comfort zone. You're trying to balance your big vision with the reality of what you can actually build and ship *right now*. Everything you've invested in is about to be revealed. It's overwhelming, I know. The difference between you and everyone else is that you will push through, like every other successful founder who has made something out of nothing.

The difference comes down to this: They shipped. Then everything changed.

The Business Side of Engineering

Engineering has a universal love language: outcomes, context, and expected experience. Whether you're hiring an engineer or doing it yourself, create a document with rules, guidelines, and truths that serves as the indisputable basis for all technical decisions. Approach every technical choice with a clear understanding of what you're trying to achieve today and in the future. What do you *know* to be absolutely true? What do you *think* might be true? The best technical decision is the one that aligns with the desired outcomes.

Sure, every founder dreams of building something that can scale flawlessly, with zero bugs, where everything can be easily changed, while being fast, compliant, and secure. As if. Realistically, everything is a game of options. Want "secure"? If that adds 20 percent to the development time, is it worth it? Compliant? Is a 30 percent increase in development time justified?

Throughout this book, I've been talking about accelerating the speed to market, achieving clock speed, getting in traffic, getting that feedback. But at what cost? That's the business side of engineering.

Your preparation—or lack thereof—becomes glaringly obvious when you enter the engineering phase. Every decision you've made, every assumption you've tested (or haven't), every conversation you've had (or avoided) with potential customers adds (or detracts) from how well you manage the business of engineering.

We will know if you've done the work. If you come into this phase with screens already mapped out, with flows, experiences, and a clear position, it shows. You'll have a level of clarity that comes only from deep understanding. But don't do it for us; do it for yourself. Confidence and clarity at this stage are your secret weapon and the best single defense against building a product no one wants, even if it's for a problem people want solved.

Learn to Lead

As if you don't already have more to do than is humanly possible, there's the massive matter of becoming a credible leader. Chances are you have come across some managers who were amazing, some who were awful, and some who didn't matter one way or another. You've got to find your own style, one you can pull off without fakery (which never succeeds for long). While you're figuring it out, here's a short list of some guiding principles and practices.

- Set clear expectations. Define what "done" looks like for each feature, each sprint, each milestone. Be specific. Be detailed. Reduce the risk of misinterpretation.

- Establish regular check-ins. Have scheduled times for updates and discussions. This gives your team uninterrupted time to work and gives you peace of mind knowing you'll be kept in the loop.

- Trust but verify. Give your team autonomy but have processes in place to review work and ensure quality. This isn't about mistrust; it's about maintaining standards and catching issues early.

- Focus on results, not methods. As long as the outcome meets your requirements and aligns with your vision, don't get hung up on how it was achieved. Your engineers are problem solvers; let them solve problems their way(ish).

- Be available but not overbearing. Be there if they need you, but don't be in the back seat asking if you are there yet. Be a resource, not a roadblock.

Steer the ship, don't row the boat. Set the direction, make the big decisions, keep everyone aligned with the vision. But let your team do what you hired them to do: build an amazing product.

The Handoff: A Blueprint

You've been nurturing this idea in your head for months, maybe years. You're about to hand it over to someone else to actually make it happen. It's your brainchild, your ticket to a new life. It's incredibly exciting because it's also totally terrifying.

This is the moment you transfer ownership of your vision to an engineer, in whatever form: through an agency, on Upwork, to a cofounder, to a friend, or even to yourself—via a contract. The handoff demands a contract with your engineer (even if that engineer is you). By contract, I mean an agreement that goes beyond a legal document. What's required is a shared understanding of expectations, responsibilities, and outcomes that you both understand and agree to. This includes how you'll work together, communicate, and measure success. Requiring yourself to make a contract forces this conversation, an amazing conversation about how you want to work together. Most founders don't do this because they're too scared or too immature to know that tough conversations aren't so tough when they happen during good times. And clarity between both parties always makes everything better.

As the product owner, you have to develop a contract clearly articulating the vision and providing context. You're obliged to deliver the assets in a manner that is clear, and of course you're obligated to make timely decisions. The engineer must agree to delivering workable solutions, flagging potential issues, and adhering to agreed-upon standards for the build, the code, and the product.

Making the effort to craft a comprehensive contract transforms what you have in your head into concrete deliverables with measurable outcomes. It makes apparent the answer to "Did I do my job?" Committing to contract terms defines the boundaries, setting you and your engineer up for a happier, healthier, more predictable and productive relationship.

Even if you are a technical founder, this still applies to you. You've got a whole other level of mindfuckery to deal with. You're not just the visionary anymore; you're the executor too. You've got to pull off the ultimate mental gymnastics move: being the business brain and the engineering hands at the same time. Your contract (with yourself) is your guide.

The challenge for the technical founder isn't the coding, obviously. The real test is in separating your two personas. Can you look at your own work with the critical eye of a founder? Can you ruthlessly prioritize features when you know exactly how cool that extra functionality (that you could build in a night's work) could be? Can you kill your own ideas when they don't serve the core vision?

The rules are the rules, whether it's you or someone else doing the work. If it is you, the rules are exponentially more important and harder to enforce.

Most founders think they can just roll into a meeting with an engineer, throw out a vision and some general direction, and the engineer will magically conjure up the perfect thing. It doesn't work like that. Not even close. For starters, there is no way anyone else could possibly understand your full vision. No matter how much you explain, write, detail, it won't be everything, complete with all the nuance, all the bits that are floating in your brain. Accept it. It's nobody's fault. This is normal. This is good. This is part of the journey.

If you want this handoff to start right, you need to have your shit together. Not the "I've got it all in my head. I can explain as we go. They will get it" wishful thinking version of together. You need the "I've got detailed workflows, screen designs, and user journeys" kind of together.

The blueprint, the package, whatever you want to call it is not just a list of features. It offers a clear statement of what you need to deliver to your audience. It's a package that you have already built for yourself if you have been steadily Earning the Right.

In the event that you glossed over the earlier chapters, here's what you should have in shareable form by now:

User stories that detail how people will interact with your product.

Wireframes that show the layout of screens you need engineered.

Flow diagrams that map out how users will navigate through your product.

A prioritized list of features that clearly shows what needs to be built first, second, third, and so on.

Technical requirements that outline any specific technologies or integrations your product needs to work with.

Having these in place means it's more likely that what gets built actually does the following:

- aligns with your vision
- solves the problem you set out to solve
- works in a manner that users want
- offers something users are willing to pay for

And you've done all this without going broke. Obsess over every user interaction. Question every assumption. Because this blueprint is at the heart of your entire product.

The Art of Not Fucking It Up

Engineers are not mind readers. They haven't been thinking about your idea for years. You can't reasonably expect them to connect all your dots and magically know your answer. They need you to communicate. Clearly. Consistently. And without the founder haze and mumblings.

Many founders make the rookie error of valuing urgency over quality. They're so eager to get things moving that they sacrifice clarity and rush through explanations, race over details, and make assumptions that lead to misunderstandings. Misunderstandings are the death of good products.

Quality over urgency. Quality. Over. Urgency. But also. Hurry. Up.

Understanding is more important than speed. There's nothing slower (or more costly) than having to redo weeks of work because of a simple, avoidable misunderstanding.

I'm offering this advice for dealing with engineering, but it is also solid CEO leadership practice. *Be crystal clear about what you want to achieve.* Don't focus on the how. Obsess about the what and the why. Keep pushing for the right outcome, context, and experience, and don't get lost in the weeds of implementation.

An outcome-focused leadership approach does two crucial things:

1. It allows your engineering team to leverage their expertise. They know the tech better than you do, so let them figure out the best way to achieve the outcomes you need.

2. It keeps you focused on what really matters: the bigger picture of solving your users' problems.

Many founders make the rookie error **of valuing urgency over quality.**

Your job now is to be the voice of the user. The guardian of the vision. The one who always, always brings the conversation back to the *problem* you're solving and the *people* you're solving it for.

This doesn't mean you don't engage in technical discussions. You absolutely should. Ask questions. Lots of questions. Not to challenge your team's expertise but to understand. Because the more you understand about the technical side, the better able you will be to make informed product decisions. There will be lots of these to make. Trade-offs to consider. Compromises to negotiate. As you are the founder, these decisions ultimately fall to you. You need to be informed enough to make the right calls but detached enough from the technical details to keep the big picture in sharp focus.

Sixty-Day Sprint

There are four rules of build: Hurry up. Don't run out of money. Take intelligent shortcuts (but understand them). Pay attention to detail. Yeah, none of this is easy.

Your challenge is to get in front of your atomic ICP in sixty days. Why? Because the market has its own voice, and the sooner you hear it, the better. Good or bad. Building is complex. Sure, it takes more than sixty days to achieve truly great stuff: design, build, testing—all that jazz takes time. But sixty days should be enough time to deliver something that can do *something*. It's what we're aiming for. What can you and your team do in that time that provides real value?

Remember, shipping isn't about perfection. It never was, and it never will be. It's about progress. It's about getting your minimum delightful experience (yes, this again) into the hands of real users. Because everything changes when actual humans get involved.

What Do You Need to Build?

You think you know what your users want? You're building the minimum amount to prove out what you know and test what you don't. These experiments validate your assumptions before and during the build process.

Choose your weapons wisely, beginning with your tech stack. This is everything from your choice of programming language to frameworks to databases to tools to other platforms: things and bits, the full set of technical choices that powers your product. Your tech stack isn't just about what's trendy or what you're comfortable with. You want what will let you move fast, break things (in a good way), and scale when you need to.

These are the things to consider:

- Scalability: Can it grow with your user base?

- Flexibility: How easy is it to add or modify features when (not if) you need to pivot?

- Community support: Is there a robust ecosystem of libraries and tools, or will you be coding everything from scratch in a silo?

And of course,

- Learning curve: Can your team (or you) become productive quickly, or will you spend the next however many weeks in learning mode?

I often cheat by periodically checking out the latest Y Combinator cohorts. A look at their tech stacks might reveal good solutions that make life easier. These tend to move like wildfire inside of accelerators, so I want to build on something known, true, and tested. I also want to see the new tools or other tech just coming into market. Choose one that's good enough and start building. Just make sure it's not the wrong one.

Oh, the wrong one! How do you know? You don't, not with 100 percent certainty, but by looking at what others in your peer group or those just ahead of you are doing, by leveraging the wisdom of the rest of the world (with a dive into Reddit), you should be able to make an informed decision based on what is working for others in similar situations. You don't need to innovate here. Granted what works for them might not be the best for you. But generally, 98 percent of your solution is not unique—only 2 percent is "snowflake." That means for the 98 percent, there should be a standard-ish answer. And if it's ubiquitous enough, there will be plenty to read about it.

Intelligent Shortcuts

LinkedIn cofounder Reid Hoffman said it best when he explained that choosing intelligent shortcuts isn't about cutting corners; it's about smart deployment of your (always) limited resources. For founders, this is especially crucial advice.

Use existing tools and services where you can. They can leapfrog development cycles, allow you to fit in more with less, and enable you to add functionality that you might not end up needing. This is especially true outside your core. Try not to custom-build anything or generate intellectual property that doesn't directly impact the core of your solution. Chances are, you're going to need some standard processes, such as the following:

- user authentication
- payment processing
- data visualization
- webhooks
- API management
- user messaging tools
- content editing services

Don't reinvent the wheel. Where possible, opt to use something that already exists in the market as either open source or affordable, which is certainly cheaper than building it from scratch. You are building your MDE to solve your users' problem, not to dazzle someone with technical feasibility. You are building to attract someone to use and pay for your solution.

Building for Change

Your first version will be wrong. The only question is how wrong. Accept it. Plan for it. Build for it. Create an architecture that's flexible and modular. Think of your product as a set of LEGO blocks that can be easily rearranged, rather than a monolithic structure that'll crumble if you try to change one tiny thing.

The goal is to make it easy to change course when (not if) you need to. Because trust me, you will need to. The market will speak, and it'll probably be saying something very different from what you expected. Keep talking to your potential customers throughout this process. So many founders think they need to wait to show their stuff, but you can offer a sneak peek: You can show some screens, some processes, some bits to your potential users. The more involved and attached prospects are to you and your journey early on, the higher the likelihood of conversion when you launch.

One important caveat: Your build strategy needs to align with your market strategy.

Are you positioning your product as a disruptor in your market (blue ocean)?

Or are you going after the established players head-on (red ocean)?

If you're disrupting, you might be able to get away with a scrappier product that serves an underserved segment. If you're competing directly in a red ocean, you have to bring your A game from day one.

Testing and Security

One of my fave lines is, "Tests are the vegetables of the coding world." You know you should do it, but it's so tempting to skip it and go straight for the dessert. Not testing your product is not an option (neither is avoiding all vegetables), so this is a question of the *acceptable* level of testing.

Strategic testing? Test the core functionality, the common user paths, and those edge cases that could cause major issues. Automate what you can, but don't get busy achieving 100 percent test coverage for a product that is inevitably going to have to undergo significant change.

You're aiming for good enough to ship, and as we discussed earlier, only you can define that.

While we're on the topic of testing, let's talk ever so briefly about security. Build with security in mind from the start. You don't have to be 100 percent perfect right out of the gate. We all share some passwords, have access to production databases, have our user data as an Excel file on our desktop. But security is like insurance or a seat belt, because how you treat your user data says a lot about you, now more than ever when protecting privacy is a strategy.

Final point on this: There are so many out-of-the-box tools that can deliver security without your needing a chief security officer—things that just work. But you need to understand what security means today. The best way to understand cybersecurity compliance frameworks such as SOC 2 is to watch some explanatory videos.

Shipping Starts the Real Clock

Shipping isn't just a technical process for the engineers; it's a mindset. From day one, you need to be thinking about how your product will actually get into users' hands. Shipping is just the beginning. It's the moment when your idea stops being just an idea and starts being a real product in the hands of real users. Even beta users, even just you.

Think about your deployment process. How does code go from there to production? You should understand that process (what it takes, how long it takes, are there any checks in it) and how and when you as a company want to ship. Probably not on a Friday night before everyone leaves for the weekend.

Users will use your product in ways you never imagined. They'll find bugs you never spotted. They'll ask for features you never considered. And that's beautiful. Let your users break some stuff.

Once you ship, you're no longer building in a vacuum. You're getting real data, real feedback, real insights. And if you have *observability* protocols in place, and you're ready to learn and adapt—now your product starts to take meaningful shape.

Clock speed kicks in when users are watching. The faster you take in feedback, make decisions, and implement changes, the faster your product will evolve. It matters because your users don't care about your vision. They don't care about your clever architecture or your innovative use of technology. They care about whether your product solves their problem. Period.

The market in the real world is messy. It's chaotic. It's unpredictable. But it's also where the magic happens. It's where you'll discover use cases you never imagined. You'll uncover problems you never knew existed. You'll find opportunities you never saw coming.

What happens after you ship is the true test of a founder. Whether you can take that initial germ of an idea of a product and evolve it into something truly valuable. Something indispensable. Something users can't imagine living without.

You'll never be "done." There will always be more to learn, more to improve, more to build. But that's the beauty of it. That's the thrill.

The Final Push

You've earned the right to ship. You've done the hard work of preparing, planning, and building. You've sweated over every detail, every decision. You have prioritized quality over urgency. Now it's time to put your creation out into the world and see what happens.

Will it be scary? Absolutely. Will there be moments of doubt, anger, disappointment, frustration, of wanting to throw in the towel? You bet. But there will also be moments of triumph. Moments when you see your product making a real difference in someone's life. Moments when you realize you're building something that matters.

So take a deep breath. Square your shoulders. You're a builder. You're a problem solver. You're a founder now. And I can't wait to see what you've created.

You've earned this moment. Welcome to the game. It's time to play.

EARN IT

- As you approach your ship date, don't start packing in more and more.
- Focus on polishing what you have.
- Do a full run-through of your product.
- Use it as your users would.
- Try to break it.
- Check your error handling. How does your product behave when things go wrong?
- Review your user onboarding process. Is it clear? Is it intuitive?
- Every second a user spends confused is a second they're not experiencing the value of your product. Make sure you're delivering the golden handshake that leads to user engagement.

10

EARN THE RIGHT TO GROW

LET'S TALK about growth. By now, I hope you're convinced that if you build it, they will not come. Although it might seem like I am once again asking you to do the impossible or at least pushing you to get way ahead of yourself. Well, maybe I am. But trust me on this. You need to start thinking about your growth strategy now.

It doesn't have to be perfect or even right, but it cannot be some afterthought you tack on once you've built your product and begin wondering, "How can I find users?" Distribution is a process you need to address now.

You've probably heard or will hear other founders talk about product-led growth (PLG). It's the "Make your product so good it sells itself!" mantra. Those who want to believe in this eagerly point at big examples. "Look at Slack! Look at Dropbox!"

The holy grail of growth is advocacy: "If I build a product that someone else advocates for, my customer acquisition cost is zero. It's like I have a free sales army." Yup.

Then there's Uber's version of the holy grail: "If I build a product that has sharing built in, not the option to 'add a user' but a feature interwoven into the product to bring in another party, then every user who arrives will bring in x more users." The examples here likely reflect your own user experience. Think about when someone sends you a Docusign, Dropbox, or Calendly link, or a Slack invite. If you have a great experience, which tool will you use when you need that functionality?

Let's go a step further. If your process for onboarding new users to try your solution, freemium, or whatever is fully frictionless, then your focus can be on driving leads, and your website and software will do the rest. Sure. Except your onboarding probably isn't going to be so fab that it does all the work for you. Most likely you'll end up combining it with lead generation.

PLG is just so *amazing*. But like many so-called holy grails, it's never quite all that. PLG, or any other XYZ growth strategy, isn't a magic bullet. It's not even a strategy. It's a tactic and a tool that is not cheap, easy, or all-powerful. A hard, cold truth is that growth without retention is just delayed churn. You're not clever for acquiring users if they all leave. You're just burning cash with extra steps. Poorly executed PLG is just that: delayed churn. All vanity and no sanity.

How do we develop an XYZ growth strategy (tactic!)? Start by answering this core question: What's the main engine driving your company's growth? Can you identify the *primary mechanism* that will attract users, drive adoption, and fuel your startup's expansion? The "XYZ" part? That's just a placeholder for whatever's leading the charge.

Why does this matter? Simple. In today's ridiculously competitive landscape, where traditional outbound marketing is hard and capturing attention is even harder, you need a real plan. Ads are expensive, people are jaded, and attention spans are getting shorter by the day. Catching your share of attention is discouragingly difficult, and it's even harder if you're the only one trying to draw some interest to what you're offering.

Here's another holy grail: inbound growth. In this scenario, users come to you, ideally at a low customer acquisition cost. XYZ growth strategies depend on a flywheel effect, where your product, your users, or your content do the heavy lifting of attracting new customers. When done right, your existing users become your best marketers. They love your product so much they invite their colleagues, and they become your evangelists. Maybe best of all, it costs you next to nothing.

We're talking about these aspects of growth strategy now because every startup has limited resources. Fueling growth requires a conversation about cash and another one about users. What you're trying to get to is the most efficient use of (your limited) capital. And you need to think about growth strategy as it relates to the product you have built.

Some Flavors of XYZ Growth

There are many flavors of growth strategies. Here's a sampling.

- Product-led growth: Your product is your primary sales tool. Great. But if your product doesn't inspire delight and doesn't evolve with user needs, it dies.

- Sales-led growth: High-touch and relationship-driven. Powerful but expensive and hard to scale.

- Community-led growth: Harness the power of your users. Awesome, if you can pull it off. But communities need constant nurturing.

- Marketing-led growth: Classic demand generation. Still relevant but increasingly expensive and noisy.

- Channel-led growth: Leverage partners to expand reach. Can be a game-changer, but you're dependent on others.

- Content-led growth: Educate and attract. Slow burn but can create lasting authority.

These are the most frequently used, but the list goes on. Sorry, but here's the kicker: You need to be actively engaged in *all* of these. Not all at once, not all equally, but they all play a role. I know. I can hear your moans. But read on. Advice and encouragement ahead.

The Missing Piece: XYZ Retention

Everyone wants to forget about consequences, about the reality that for every action there is an equal and opposite reaction. When it comes to *growth* motion, you need a corresponding *retention* strategy. This is where most founders fuck up. They're so focused on getting users in the door, they forget to lock it behind them ("lock" in the most gentle and friendly way).

Think about it. You have worked hard to create this entire sequence of motions that drives people to do the thing you want them to do, namely, start the customer journey. You make it epic and that's what you are tracking. Getting them to get started. Your focus and associated costs are on these inbound opportunities, because the wind, sailing with you, is just the best feeling.

But if you want to keep that wind in your sails, you must spend at least equal time, if not more, on your retention strategy. Obviously, retention strategy with no growth is not a thing, so "more" doesn't mean do it first; it just means "more."

Think back to the various options for growth strategy and look at what happens when we pair them with retention. Something like this:

- Product-led growth needs product-led retention. It's not enough to have great onboarding. Your product needs to become indispensable.

- Sales-led growth needs relationship-led retention. Those high-touch sales need equally high-touch account management.

- Community-led growth needs community-led retention. Foster belonging and create value beyond your product.

You get the idea. Acquisition without retention is like trying to fill a leaky bucket. You can pour faster or you can fix the leak. Do both.

Design for Growth and Experimentation

This is uncomfortable. I'm asking you to think about your growth and retention strategies before you have a proven product. The reason is less about forcing you to take a position, although you should. Even more important is thinking

Acquisition without retention is like trying to fill a leaky bucket. **You can pour faster or you can fix the leak. Do both.**

about how such a position might impact you. It would simply be awful if you did the thinking after you had a product.

We say it often and we always mean it, especially at the start: Absolutely no one knows what the fuck they are doing. The winners are the ones who can figure it out the fastest. This is experimentation, again and again, because your entire founder's journey is one step away from putting on a white lab coat.

If we agree that customer acquisition is the thing, we will probably agree that your first few hypotheses for acquiring users could be wrong. Next, we have to agree that your job is to be less wrong over time. The best way to be less wrong is to have a system to create a view, design a quick and cheap test, measure some result, and double down on what works. Relentless experimentation.

Double. Down. On. What. Works.

Run faster than your competition. That's the competitive advantage.

Bullshit

There's a ton of growth-hacking bullshit about the founder's journey. Vanity metrics. Growth at all costs. "Best practices" that are neither best nor practiced. If there was a killer growth hack, it wouldn't be shared. People generally don't give away their competitive advantages. Forget the noisy distractions of cheap advice and false promises. Stay focused on the three things that matter.

1. Sustainable growth: If your growth relies on unsustainable tactics (buying users, burning cash on ads), you're building a house of cards.

2. True north metrics: Focus on the numbers that actually matter. Revenue. Retention. Lifetime value. Not bullshit vanity metrics like app downloads or logo count.

3. Unit economics: Understand the true cost of acquiring and retaining a customer. If you're losing money on every user, you can't make it up in volume.

Before you write a single line of code, before you hire a single salesperson, before you spend a dime on marketing, you need to have a clear vision of how you think you're going to grow. Because if you can't see that path, you're not building a business. You're just fucking around with a product idea.

EARN IT

So here's the advice and encouragement I promised earlier, in the form of some questions you should be thinking about. If you can answer these, you're on your way to figuring out growth. (Don't worry about the right answers and make your most informed guess.)

1 Virality: How does your product naturally encourage sharing? Is it built into the core experience?

2 Expansion: What's your land-and-expand strategy? How does use of your product create opportunities for upselling?

3 Network effects: Does your product become more valuable as more people use it? If not, why not?

4 Friction reduction: How easy is it for new users to get value? Can you create a "wow" moment in the first x seconds (see chapter 8)?

5 Data leverage: Are you collecting the right data to fuel personalization, improve the product, and drive retention?

These aren't nice-to-haves. Find any product, anywhere, that seems to be doing something right and see how they are executing an XYZ growth strategy. It's probably how you found this book, either directly, by referral, or by some partner strategy that put it in front of you.

11

EARN THE RIGHT TO (NOT) LAUNCH

NO ONE CARES. It's not like you launch and the market stops what it's doing, racing over to see your announcement. It's not like your launch will suddenly cut through the noise and ads to grab the attention of the market. No. No one will care unless you make them care. Care is earned. Launching is just the first step in dragging your initial few customers—the ones who want to be your customers but need to be found, sold, and promised—over the finish line.

The worst thing about launching is that it's the first time in this journey when something is truly out of your hands. After launch you cannot control if someone buys, loves, or stays. You can do everything in your power to try to deliver that incredible delight, but it's no longer in your control and that's a scary realization. Earning the right to launch requires stepping out of the safe space of development and into the harsh light of the real market. Don't do it until you've built a foundation that will give your launch a fighting chance of success, one customer at a time.

Big Versus Small Letter L Launch

Let's just start with the truth. The Launch—whatever that means to you—is mostly for you. I get it. Having a hard stop, a real deadline, something to work towards unifies and motivates you and your team. After months of slog, we all need an actual milestone to celebrate. And that's okay. But don't expect anything to happen just because you've flipped the sign on your door from Closed to Open.

I 100 percent understand the appeal of The Launch fantasy. If you execute a solid launch moment, orchestrate a clever marketing campaign, get featured on the right tech blog, get waves of engagement on your LinkedIn post, then customers will flood in. You'll grab some virality. Investors will be throwing money at you. You'll be a founder for real, and it'll be smooth sailing from there.

Here's an alternative approach that might serve you better, but it is tough to do, because we all need a major milestone. Don't launch in the grand manner. Just get your product out there in a very small way.

When you have a product that's (mostly) ready, find one prospect who wants your solution. One. Onboard them personally, giving them the most magical, white-glove experience possible. Learn from that interaction. Curate the onboarding experience. Find the bugs. Correct that typo on your landing page. Pay obsessive attention to the details. Then find one more customer and do it all over again. And again. And again.

If you can restrain yourself from big gestures, commit to executing a series of small launches. Let each one build on the last, slowly gaining firm traction and momentum. Fight and claw for every single user, every bit of attention, every scrap of market share incrementally—that's what a real launch strategy that matters looks like.

Acquiring users one by one is not glamorous. There are no splashy press releases or extravagant launch parties. But it's hyper-effective because all your energy is focused on getting five users and learning everything you can from them. Your intensely personal sherpa-ing of these early customers will likely buy you some slack when things break (as they will). Wouldn't it be amazing when you finally do launch to have some genuine ass-kicking testimonials? And some solid user data?

By not capital-*L* launching and working instead to get your product into the hands of a small number of users, you can avoid the pitfall of false expectations while waiting for the market to notice you. Instead, it's just you and some genuine users, building momentum and your business, steadily and sustainably.

Your goal right now is not to onboard thousands of users. Honestly, you have no idea if you could even manage that. It would probably be a shit show. Your job now is to delight tens of users so thoroughly that they can't help but spread the word. That's how you truly earn the right to scale.

When you think you're ready to launch, consider reframing it in your mind. It's not a single one-day big event. Think of it as the start of real work, the beginning of a careful, intentional process of bringing your solution to the world, one delighted user at a time. It's the starting gun in a marathon that only you can hear. All the work you've done to get you to this point, every sacrifice, every dollar, everything has brought you to the starting line. The party comes later.

What's Your Story?

What have you done besides developing your product to prep for market entry? Humans love a good story. We remember them better than we remember features. Every single motherfucker out there is saying the same thing: "We are the best; we have exceptional customer support; our app integrates to the stack; it is highly secure, has great features, is the best price." Every. Single. Startup. What are you saying? The same thing? Can't you find a better story? Dedicate yourself to crafting a legit narrative around your product that resonates on an emotional level.

Learn to frame your startup's journey and your product's value in a way that connects with people. Your story is so specific to who and what you are as a founder, but I will tell you, it's why founders are the best and worst sales reps. Most of you can't sell for shit, you're awful at outbound, even more terrible at closing, *but* you know the market, the competition, the problem, and the solution, and that makes you the absolute best at selling. That's part of your story.

Skip the BS. Potential customers know your platform is built on a shoestring. WTF, you're a startup! So cast a vision for the future, publish your road map, your view of the market, because most customers are coming to you now because they want to be on the journey *with* you. That's even more interesting to them than thinking you have all the solutions right now.

Show, Don't Tell

A clever young founder told me recently that there were three traits he believed he needed to attract top talent and investors. His list? Leadership. Vision. Ability to execute. Brilliant.

Listing them is the easy part. I asked him, "What have you done to demonstrate, to show beyond any doubt that you've got these critical abilities?" Crap. He thought hard and came up with a few mumbles. Starting right then, he had a new lens for deciding what was important. He had to choose actions that proved he had the traits he knew he needed to succeed. His list is not the only "right" list. Your list may be different. What's important is asking yourself the question, "What do I have to be able to do to increase my chances of success?" And being dead honest in your answer.

As a founder, you already have too many things that need to be done. Too many decisions, too many unknowns, too few resources. I get that. Weigh how you invest in yourself, how you allocate your resources, and how you spend your precious time. Honestly assess if what you are doing is minimizing your chances of failure. Are you working at becoming the CEO you need to be?

Top talent and savvy investors are looking to see what you have done, not what you hope to do. Your job is to use your actions to prove you're CEO material.

Build in Public

This is super-scary stuff, but it works for some so it's worth considering. Building in public means sharing your startup journey openly and honestly with the world as you go. Pulling back the curtain and letting people see the messy, imperfect process of building a company. Sure, there are risks to be managed, but here are some upsides.

- It creates investment. Not financial investment (yet) but emotional investment. People who follow your journey feel like they're part of it. They're rooting for you to succeed.

- It builds trust. Transparency breeds trust. When you're open about your challenges and failures as well as your successes, people see you as authentic and relatable.

- It provides valuable feedback. By sharing your process, you invite input from a wide range of sources. You might get valuable insights or connections that you wouldn't have otherwise.

- It creates content. Every step of your journey is a potential blog post, tweet, or LinkedIn update. This constant stream of content keeps you top of mind for your audience.

- It attracts talent and investors. People want to work with and invest in founders who are passionate and have a clear vision. Building in public showcases these qualities.

We all have mixed views about this approach. Some hate the founders who are only about fame and brand-building, especially when they are touting themselves as the brand. If fame is the point, move on. If generating influence and interest for your startup is the point, then make time to be at every relevant conference and every industry-related event, talking the talk. Then get back in your basement and continue to build (maybe altered by what you've heard at those events!).

Raise Your Army of Advocates

Remember all those conversations you never had while validating your problem and solution because you were sure you already knew the answer? You didn't need validation, and you just knew it was a waste of time to talk to strangers. I totally

Learn to frame your startup's journey and your product's value **in a way that connects with people.**

understand and agree. Except. All those potential customers you could have spoken to, listened to, humbled yourself before and asked for guidance or their view? That's the army of advocates you could have been building.

Anybody who has been on the journey with you from the beginning now understands the problem you're solving. They have seen you evolve, grow, listen, and engage (your monthly newsletter did that for you). They are that one extra Like or Comment or Share or something, because that *one* might be all you need to get something going.

There is no better marketing than influence or a referral, even one kinda passionate user singing your praises is worth more than all your ads. You don't need superfans to actively sell for you or scream from the rooftops, but their support is incredibly valuable. Who are your advocates?

The Regret Era

Sorry to close on a downer, but welcome to the Regret Era. The moment just before launch when you suddenly realize all the things you could have—should have—done in the past 30, 90, or 120 days to move the needle and you didn't. It's fine. Well, it's not fine; that's why it's called "regret." Plus, what you didn't/wouldn't/couldn't do has already cost you time and money.

Let's talk about some of these missed opportunities and how you might still capitalize on them.

Nurture your newsletter. If you haven't been sending regular updates to your early supporters and interested parties, start now. It's never too late to begin keeping your people close and involved. Even a simple monthly email sharing your progress, challenges, and wins can go a long way in building engagement.

Think about it. As you have gone through this adventure you've met people with varying degrees of interest. Imagine if each month you had sent an update, even a short investor update with progress, status, screens, a question, an ask. Sure, most may ignore your messages, even unsubscribe, but you don't need most. You need one: one investor, one customer, one partner, or just one person to reply.

Get in traffic. Every call, every meeting, every interaction with potential users or industry players is a chance to build your network and your mailing list. If you've been heads-down in development, it's time to stop hiding behind your laptop and start having conversations.

Build your personal brand. In the early days of a startup, you are your brand. If you've been operating in stealth mode, you can imagine my views on closely protecting your precious idea. Who the hell do you think actually cares? Consider shifting to a "build in public" approach.

Share your journey on LinkedIn, X, or your blog. When you do make that launch announcement, you want a network that's ready to amplify your message. Building in public is not perfect for everyone, and it can be quite draining and time-consuming. You still have to maintain focus on your product. But if building in public helps you reach your customer, it's worth the investment.

I know your eighteen followers on LinkedIn are not begging for your updates. Go ahead anyway and create a cadence, follow it, fight the lack of engagement. Chances are it will grow *if* you deliver value.

Ignite the outbound engine. Have you built a system for reaching out to your prospects? Have you considered how to capture your competitors' audience versus creating your own? Are you contemplating an outbound email campaign or targeted ads to a specific LinkedIn or Facebook group to grab your competitors' audience? Worth a try since this is an audience your competitors have spent money educating. See if you can't attract some of its attention.

Activate your advocates. What happened to those early supporters, potential partners, analysts, and industry influencers you talked to during your validation phase? Or the people you identified but never reached out to? If what you say is reasonable and valuable, clever execs and great leaders will engage. Everyone likes to look like a thought leader on the front of the tech transformation. An amazing data point about some of the greatest founders is that they are the greatest cold-emailers. It's bananas who they get to respond because they made the effort to be interesting.

Create content that drives SEO. I'm admittedly a bigger fan of SEO than most. I get the need to avoid investing in long-form content for a product that may not be around or may change drastically, but SEO tactics do work. Have a marginal strategy, then take a tiny allocation of time to write into your keywords.

Party with purpose. Have you been showing up in startup founder networks? I dislike most of them. If you are a founder at a founders' event, what's there for you? Better to go back in your basement and work on your product. However, there is value in other groups that aren't just founders swapping stories. Join the groups where more value is on offer, whether that's advice, support, stack info, or a thing you need, like the customer who asked for your master service agreement (MSA) or the customer who wants you to get SOC 2 certification. It sure would be nice to have someone to ask who knows more than you.

> ## EARN IT
>
> There's no such thing as a life lived without regret, so I'm not asking you to tackle all seven suggestions. Take *one* from the regret list and fix it now. Your choice. Which one is going to move the needle most?

12

EARN THE RIGHT TO SELL

YOU'VE BUILT SOMETHING. Maybe it's great. But it doesn't matter how great it is if you can't convince anyone to use it. The days of building something fantastic and "Boom!" the business rockets are close to nonexistent. Now your best opportunity is DIY startup sales, aka founder-led sales. All through this book, I've been urging and encouraging you to do as much as you can by yourself. I know. When you're trying to do something new, it's always messy and hard. But for startups, founder DIY is shockingly important. So stay with me and get ready to start demystifying the sales process.

Let's break it down to the three elements of founder-led sales you need to master: approach, tactics, and of course, pricing.

1. Approach

This isn't about being a slick salesperson or mastering some secret selling trick. It's a mindset about owning the early sales process because as the founder, no one, no matter how many years in the sales trenches they've logged, is better suited to sell your product. Don't outsource your early sales. Founder-led sales aren't optional components of the journey; they are a mandate. Doing it yourself, at least initially, is the fastest way to learn what works, what doesn't, and how to position your product to solve real problems. Put yourself in traffic with potential customers to help you learn, understand, and feel their pain.

You will struggle with getting the ball rolling (sales prospecting, deal origination) or feel awkward talking about money (closing), but when it comes to understanding the product and solving real problems, this is where your strengths align perfectly with the customer's needs. And that's why you are, for now, the best person to be selling your product.

No matter how many sales goals someone has blown past in their career, they can't match your crazy unique strengths. Your deep understanding of the problem, your passion for the solution, and your ability to paint a vivid vision of exactly where you are going add up to a pitch that is difficult for a prospect to ignore, despite all your non-salesperson flaws.

Your true goal in these first few closes is not the revenue. You're here to be a problem solver, a visionary—don't push hard to sell. By listening and responding, you help your customers buy. *The best salespeople are problem solvers for customers.* This is a mega mindset shift. Stop celebrating all the amazing features your product has and being deflated when deals don't close. Treat the early sales process less like a painful chore and more like a way to extend what you're already doing: listening, iterating, and using new insights to build something great that people want.

The primary pillar of founder-led sales isn't the sale itself; it's the awareness playbook that precedes it. You are the only thing that can overcome market skepticism. The market has seen plenty of fast-talking founders before, so the market demands proof. The skepticism, the ghosting, the everything awful you'll face as you learn to sell is healthy, fair, and to be expected. It's the market asking you to show why it should risk anything on you.

Don't call it rejection. It's a request for evidence. Potential buyers need to believe that betting on you won't get them fired. Better yet, choosing you will make them a hero. The hard truth is that it is just easier not to do business with you. Every answer you give, every moment of preparation tells them if you're worth their risk. Quite reasonably, people want solutions but not at any cost. If you can't walk this line between claiming it, proving it, and living it, the market won't even consider you.

Get in the Game

Success in founder-led sales is 98 percent about showing up ready, responsive, and relentless. Founders fuck this up all the time by failing to recognize that their biggest advantage is speed and their ability to move faster than the market.

Your incumbent competitors have inertia on their side. They can afford to be slow, to be cautious, to qualify prospects, and to delay process like a grown-up company. They can rely on reputation, contracts, and established process to keep customers in place. You don't have that. You're only in the game if you are reliably right there for your prospect when and how they need you. It shows in the speed of your response time, the provision of information, the turnaround of requests, the doing the work to be an incredible partner that excites your prospect.

Too often, founders think that to be taken seriously they have to act like the big boys. So they add sales qualification steps or a pre-call. They introduce friction as if speaking to them is a prize. They send an unhelpful Calendly invite offering fifteen minutes of their precious time. No problem, you do you, if you think that's how you show a prospect that you are ready to crush it for them.

Founders who win show up fully, keep the intensity high, and make the status quo feel more painful than the risk of becoming your customer. Move fast. Be the first. Get the demo ready. Be of service. To them.

See With Buyer's Eyes

Picture this: You're looking at an image that could be either a duck or a rabbit, depending on how you perceive it. This is the rabbit-duck illusion, and it's a perfect metaphor for startup sales.

You might see a rabbit—your amazing product—but your customer sees a duck—their existing problems and solutions. You can shout "Rabbit!" all you want, but they still see a duck. Your job isn't to convince them to see the rabbit; it's to show them how your rabbit solves their duck problems. Don't get lost talking about features. Show the relief, efficiency, results they'll get. In their language, paint the better future they care about, not what you think they should care about. Your job here is empathy; it's listening until you actually understand the future they want.

Remember those conversations you should have had during problem validation? The ones where you were supposed to listen more than talk? This is where that investment pays off. Storytelling becomes your secret weapon. Not polished slides or fancy demos. Your job is to help them see themselves overcoming their challenges with your solution as the tool that makes it possible.

The most compelling stories paint a picture of possibility, of transformation. That's what you're doing here: helping your prospects see a better future for themselves.

Most buying decisions aren't rational; they're psychological (we cover that in the pricing section). Customers buy because the product fits their perception of *value*, not necessarily its cost. They want to know they're making the right decision, and your job is to show them that value beyond numbers.

Frame your pitch in outcomes, not features. How much pain does your product remove? How much opportunity does it unlock? Speak to their self-interests; you have to know why the person who is buying wants to buy. Help them understand how to convert the cost of your product into the value it delivers.

2. Tactics

Nothing you've built matters if you can't get anyone's attention. Sales today isn't about blasting out messages; it's about knowing where to place your voice to actually be heard. That means getting creative, strategic, and, frankly, scrappy. Figure out how to grab the mic.

Your ideal customer isn't waiting for you. They're bombarded, distracted, and busy. So where are the shortcuts? Where do your prospects hang out, whom do they listen to, and what can get you heard above the noise? Every channel, every partnership, every platform where your customers are should be fair game. Get there. Get heard. Because you can't win deals you aren't considered for.

Your entire objective is getting a share of one powerful microphone. There are a million pathways to finding that one, but you have to try all of them to find out how to get your customer to know you exist. Do it without burning your cash on education or advertising, since you don't have the time or the budget to spend months educating the market.

Hijack the work someone else has already done to bring your audience together. You know your ICP. You've mapped your ecosystem. You know where your customers congregate. How can you overlay this existing audience to hijack the microphone? This is leveraging partnerships in your ecosystem: finding someone who introduces you to someone otherwise unreachable.

Partners lend you a voice on their trusted microphone. It's the essence of partnerships.

Part of hijacking or capturing the audience, part of grabbing the microphone is understanding you don't need your own audience if you can use someone else's. Your solution doesn't live in isolation; it's part of an ecosystem. Identify where you fit in that ecosystem, what your product can do for their audiences, who they already trust, what services they already pay for. These are your gateways.

The right partnerships give you scale without the cost. Where does your audience already go for insight or support? Find ways to align with those partners so that you show up where customers already are. Your goal isn't to compete with established players; it's to get introduced to their networks. This is how you grow trust without years of groundwork.

What company would benefit to bring you in, either directly via services or via its marketplace, or as an adjacent play, an innovation play? Who would gain by going to your atomic ICP and introducing you? Just for clarity, your "I'll give them 15 percent" of the deal is not the return they're looking for.

More Pirate Moves

Founders love to obsess over creating demand. But in the early stages, creating demand is expensive, time-consuming, and offers at best a low return. Instead, work to capture what's already there.

The problem you solve is one customers already know they have. Your competitors have spent the money on educating the market for you. Show up, faster and better, with a compelling story that tells customers why choosing you is worth a conversation. Don't try to reinvent their problem. Hijack the demand that exists and position yourself to be heard. You don't need to be the next big idea. You just need to be in the running.

Selling from Zero

You've got nothing. Absolute zero. No revenue, usage, testimonials, social proof, track record, references, simulations, transactions completed, implementations, integrations, escalations. Would you buy from you?

You have no choice. Embrace the newness. Position yourself as the underdog who's laser-focused on their problem. That doesn't mean sloppy and understaffed; it means fresh, better, stronger. Don't pretend to be more established than you are. What buyers care about more than anything is if you, the founder, will bleed for them, be relentless about getting it right *for them*.

Newness has advantages. Direct access to you, impact on the road map, exclusivity, responsiveness, and agility that no big player can match. Don't apologize for your size. You're agile, lean, adaptable, focused, and a real business. This is not an experiment. You must ensure you're on equal footing on security, privacy, public road map, support,

The best salespeople are **problem solvers for customers.**

and API, but stop trying to look big. Make being small look powerful.

All you want to do with these first sales is build proof your product works and ideally make some money along the way, enough for it not to be a free trial. Enough to tell the next prospect how well it is working for someone else.

Find me a successful founder and they will show you the text messages they are *still* getting from one of their early customers. That's the real deal. Because these people said yes in the early days, you are forever in their debt, and you should be.

Customer Success

What is customer success? What does it mean for your organization? What does it mean for revenue? And how is it measured, judged, valued? Maybe you can't answer all these questions yet. What matters is that you obsess over customer success to ensure absolute customer satisfaction, knowledge, feature expansion, and anything else you can be doing to be amazing.

Does the customer have an escalation path? Does the customer have clarity of how this will work, the timeline, the expectations? This capability to show a future customer that you are ready for them goes miles. You offer no surprises. They know how choosing you will shake out. Everyone knows you are going to land the plane as you are building the runway, but your prospects expect the detailed plan for you to win their trust.

Conversational Judo

I have a Post-it note permanently stuck to my computer screen. It just reads: "Shut the fuck up." This should be rule number one for salespeople. It's hard, especially when you're nervous and inexperienced. But when you start talking to prospects, don't be too quick to respond to every comment.

Of course, you should respond to what your customers say—just not the way you think you should. When their first reaction is "it's too expensive," your nearly irresistible instinct might be to drop the price, hoping to salvage the deal. If you immediately lower your price, you've already lost. You've agreed with the customer and devalued everything your product stands for. How about when they ask for a feature you don't have? You scramble to tell them it's on the road map. You're doing the same thing here: namely, losing control of the conversation.

Don't cave. Don't get emotional. Don't rush to defend yourself or your product. Instead, ask more questions.

When their first response is "your price is too high," don't defend or drop it. Acknowledge their concern by asking, "I understand pricing is a concern. What's the most important outcome you're looking for that would justify that level of investment?" The rhythm of the dialogue is acknowledge, repeat, ask.

If they say they need to "check with the team," don't just end the call. Ask more questions. "What are the biggest concerns your team members might have?" or "What's the most important factor for your team in making this decision?" Every objection is an opportunity to uncover more about the real issue at hand. And maybe provide the customer with the exact information they need to "sell" the team for you.

The goal is not to block the customer's force. My sales trainer years ago likened it to judo. Take the energy coming at you and redirect it back into a conversation that keeps you in control. You don't answer objections to eliminate them. That's defense. You answer objections to understand them.

Offense. You don't change their mind by agreeing with whatever shortcomings they raise. You change minds by engaging in a deeper conversation based on genuine listening.

By answering your customer's questions with curiosity instead of defensiveness, you turn objections into leverage. Keep probing, keep listening, keep learning and engaging. That's how you win (sell!).

Doubts Are Deal Crushers

Most deals die before they even get started, killed by silent objections. They think you're too new, too small, not secure enough, not established. Address every objection up front, in big colorful lights, not as objections but framed as solutions— this is not you opening with a speech on why they can't buy you; it's telling them why they can and giving them the clues, the data, the security up front.

The more you can combat internal bias, the more it becomes a fair fight. Open with a trust and safety slide. For example, you can say, "We are currently going through our ISO 27001 certification; we just completed penetration testing (pen test); we just did x or y or z." Regardless of whom you're selling to, the point is to be aware of their unspoken fears and overcome them, because the worst is a prospect that just leaves the store for reasons you can't figure out.

Saying No

Desperation kills deals. Sometimes, the right answer is to walk away. The wrong customers will demand resources you don't have, drag you away from your core, and churn the moment things get tough. There's a wave of predatory and shitty early adopters that turn startups into their personal development shop, over-expecting, pushing, and pushing. Usually these are the same ones that demand net 90 on your invoice.

Fuck 'em. But if you can't, and for many of you, that choice might not exist, just know a bad deal can kill a company. You need to ensure the price is worth it, either the price they are paying or the price of what you get out of it.

3. Pricing

Oh, the awful moment of truth. Hanging a price tag on your creation. You're staring at that blank space on your website where the price should go. The gauntlet you imagine of figuring out what people will actually pay for this thing is not actually a gauntlet. It's just a decision. Not irrevocable. A decision and a number you can adjust as you learn. So, founder, exhale. You can do this.

Every founder faces the pricing dilemma. Too high, you scare customers away. Too low, you devalue everything. You've likely heard the models: value-based, seat-based, usage-based, outcome-based, tiered, freemium. All of it is exciting and mostly irrelevant. Today, none of the models matter. What matters is getting your first paying customers and, by that very act, validating that people really will pay for your solution.

It's so easy to be overwhelmed by the nuances of pricing, the choices that sound great on paper as they point your pathway to riches. What you really need is clarity, confidence, and a simple framework. The only pricing model you need right now is one that gets you to your first paying customers, with the least amount of friction and founder anxiety.

Fallacies

Let's get two big, fat misconceptions out of the way.

1. Cheaper is better.
2. One absolute "right price" exists.

Cheaper

Founders love to lean on the belief that using the "cheaper, faster, better" line to describe their product is a sure sales closer. Buyers know such things generally don't exist, and it's not the reason a customer buys. Everyone says they are the best, everyone saves time, everyone says they're secure. These generic benefits don't stand out because they're expected and ignored.

Cheaper is in reality a red flag. Cheaper rarely works in your favor. It signals risk and suggests cutting corners. Customers know the expense associated with bringing in a new vendor; the associated switching costs such as migration, integration, training all extract a cost. So actually, for the first few years, your solution is more expensive. Cheaper does not make someone rip out an existing solution if the pain of switching exceeds the savings. So don't go there.

Right Price

The one absolute "right price" doesn't exist because price is always dictated by the market and what it is willing to pay for the value you deliver at this time. Don't worry about the whole market right now. You're focused on the tiny sliver of the market you want to enter. The ones willing to take a chance. Your first totally awesome paying customers.

Regardless of what price you set, it is a hypothesis ready to be tested. You need a starting point. The stakes are quite low because right now you don't have the audience, the volume, or the traction for anyone to notice (or care) if you get it wrong. Keep it simple.

1. Start at the low end of normal. Find a comparable product your customer buys and price similarly.
2. Then adjust 20 percent above or below. Above if you've got something game-changing; below if you're still proving yourself.

Use this as your default model if you want to end the anxious conversation you've been running in your head. Stop spinning in useless circles of worry.

Ultimately, your goal is to reach a point where your product is good enough to support a single price that is simple, predictable, and so aligned with its value that all these other pricing and sales tactics are irrelevant. Pricing is a tool enabling you to test your market, gain early traction, get feedback, and prove that people will pay for the value you promise to deliver. The psychology, the mechanics, all of it is designed to give you a slight edge. Not to manipulate or trick people but to get those first dollars in the door.

If you're already in the market and thinking about lowering your price, know this: Lowering your price is essentially bribing people to buy what you sell. It's negotiating with yourself, and it's a dangerous game. *Lowering your price is the most expensive way to get customers.* You're losing potential revenue; worse, you're essentially devaluing your entire offering by signaling your product isn't worth it. What's the cost of that?

Founders are just awful about talking price and next steps with customers; you have no idea how the customer will respond, so you say a number and then qualify it, or you say a number and then give a speech about something unrelated. Talk about money. Say the number. Show it is a worked-out number and then stop.

No excuses, no immediate discounts. For fuck's sake, don't apologize: Show why it's the price and listen to your customer. If they think you're overpriced, they're not understanding the value, and that's on you to communicate. Unless of course, you are overpriced.

Be ready to negotiate but never discount without a reason. If you're going to drop your price, get something of value in return: a case study, a referral, a longer commitment. If some percentage of your customers doesn't think you are too expensive, then you are too cheap.

Here's a counterintuitive piece of advice I picked up years ago and repeatedly have seen work: When in doubt, raise your prices. Maybe it won't work, but if it does, it's way more valuable than getting sales by lowering your price. Most firsttime founders will start low because they don't feel they've earned a higher price. But what if you're wrong? What if people will pay more? Don't preemptively make that decision for them. The market will decide.

B2X

It doesn't matter whether you're selling envelopes, AI video editing, healthcare resource planning, a developer platform, or a new social network. The principles of pricing are universal. Whether you're selling to a solo entrepreneur, a small team, or a Fortune 500 organization, the core rules stay the same: *Pricing is about the value you deliver and how well you communicate that value.*

Sure, enterprise customers might ask for your SOC 2 or HIPAA compliance documentation before they buy. They might want to discuss the MSA and have their IT team looped in. And yes, if you're targeting consumers, you'll be considering freemium models, one-click payments, and virality or growth hacks. It's easy to believe these factors define your pricing decisions, but they don't. You don't need to have all the answers on day one. You don't need to solve every compliance hurdle or every contract detail, or predict every customer objection.

Whether your customers are consumers, enterprises, or small businesses, they make purchasing decisions based on whether the value of your product outweighs the cost to them, including the cost of dealing with you as an early-stage startup. That means you. The risk you present, the inexperience and the uncertainty you bring. So respond to everything you can, but ultimately, pricing is about getting them to say yes.

That's how pricing works, whether your deals close in minutes or after months of negotiation. It's true that the more artillery you have to show your prospective customer your value as both a product and a company, the easier it is to get to that yes. But that's not a pricing conversation, that's a core product conversation.

Make It Binary

Just for today, just for right now, think of pricing as a binary decision. Does your pricing align with the value you're delivering? Yes or no. Can you explain to me why or how your pricing is correct? Can you take me through how you quantified value? No, of course not, because pricing is both an art and a science. First-time founders are usually charging too low because they have not yet figured out how to articulate their value well enough.

Your customer doesn't care about your costs, time, effort, anything. They care about what your product does for them, period. Their perception of value is based on what they gain by solving a problem, not what you lose by providing a solution.

If you're scrambling to figure out pricing just as you're about to launch, you've probably got bigger problems. It means you haven't spent enough time in traffic talking to potential customers. Pricing is an outcome of being in traffic, a direct reflection of your understanding of your ideal customer. Whom did you build the product for? Did you ever have the courage to ask about price?

If you didn't get in traffic, you're likely running a "keep the lights on" or "don't scare them away" pricing playbook, trying to find a sweet spot with no real data. Which means you'll underprice because you're a founder who is unsure you can justify a price that feels a touch uncomfortable.

To make matters worse, if you don't have enough leads, you cannot run experiments. You're feeling pressure to hit a 100 percent close rate. You don't have budget to scare off a prospect for any reason. If that's your situation, everything around the price needs to be perfect, not just the price, but trust, transparency, complexity—these all matter. Your customers have bought software before; they understand value, and they know the playbook.

You want to move the needle a fraction towards you, instead of against you. When you're selling to experienced buyers, if you adhere to the following five rules, the customer is more likely to buy than to be scared off. Maybe. And that's all we want. To move the needle a fraction towards us versus against us.

1. Sell how your customer buys. Meet them where they are, how they are used to purchasing. If they use seats, consumption, or storage, mirror that. It's one less thing for them to have to understand.

2. Anchor to the expected. Your customer has bought similar tech before. They have a mental price point. Start there. Go higher if you're truly revolutionary; lower to reflect your newness.

3. Do not price innovate. Complex or weird pricing models confuse and alienate. Stick to simple, transparent pricing that's easy to understand. Innovate on your product, not on pricing.

4. Avoid greed. Don't burn a great prospect with unnecessary implementation or service fees or gotchas. Your customers are clever; they'll walk.

5. Enable async buying. You're losing customers without even knowing it. They come to your website, can't find clear answers, get hit with a forced sales call or asked to trade their email for your shitty ebook. Get rid of it. Just give them the information they need, when they need it: clear pricing, FAQs, self-serve demos, live chat (without email). Make it easy for them to buy on their terms. Not yours.

Perhaps the best rule of startup pricing is if they have to ask a question about your pricing, you have introduced friction. And as soon as you introduce friction, you make it easier for them to not buy.

Brain Games

You kind of know some of the weird psychology of pricing so let's take a look at some of the common tactics. Not because you're going to run these playbooks, but because it's always useful to be reminded that we are all influenced to some extent by psychological pricing ploys. Pricing isn't just about numbers: It's about perception, emotion, and the weird quirks of our brain.

The first tactic is the *price-quality bias*. People tend to associate higher prices with higher quality. This doesn't mean you should jack up your prices to ridiculousness. But it does mean that being the cheapest option isn't always the advantage you may think it is.

Second is the *power of 9*. Prices ending in 9 (such as $99 instead of $100) have been shown to increase sales. It's irrational, but it works. However, if you're positioning yourself as a premium product, round numbers can actually be more effective. It's all about context.

Anchoring is another powerful tool. By presenting a higher price point first, you can make your actual price seem more reasonable. This is why you often see those "valued at *x* dollars" claims next to the actual, lower price.

And don't forget about the *decoy effect*. By introducing a third option that's clearly inferior, you can guide customers towards the option you actually want them to choose. This is why you often see those "middle" tiers that seem to offer the best value. We know this works, because you probably choose the middle option at the gas pump.

But perhaps the most important psychological factor in pricing is *loss aversion*. People are more motivated by the fear of losing something than by the prospect of gaining something of equal value. This is why framing your price in terms of what the customer stands to lose by not using your product can be so effective.

The way you present pricing impacts customer perception and absolutely influences buying decisions. Anchoring, framing, scarcity, decoy—once you know these tactics, you see them everywhere. And let's not forget the price-ending-in-9 trick that still works on you and everybody else.

This is all interesting and useful to know, but at the beginning, it's way too easy to get caught up in psychological tactics instead of your core focus to find one customer willing to buy.

Pricing Models and Testing

There's a smorgasbord of pricing models out there and choosing the right one likely will not make or break your startup. You don't have to pick one. Many startups use a hybrid approach. Maybe you have a tiered subscription model with some consumption-based elements. Or a freemium model with outcome-based pricing for enterprise clients. Just don't make it so complex you confuse your customers.

Align your pricing model with how your product delivers value. If your product saves time, maybe usage-based pricing makes sense. If it drives revenue, perhaps an outcome-based model is worth considering. Here are some popular options.

- Subscription-based: Charge a recurring fee for access. Easy, predictable. But churn is always a threat.

- Consumption-based: Charge based on usage (seats, actions). It's fair but less predictable.

- Outcome-based: Charge based on results. Hardest to implement but aligns pricing with value.
- Freemium: Basic version free, charge for premium. Good for user acquisition but conversion is hard.
- Flat rate: Simple and scalable. Predictable for customers but may undercharge heavy users.

You're going to get your pricing wrong. Everyone does. The key is to treat pricing as an ongoing experiment, not a one-time decision. Start with your best guess, based on all the factors you know, use data (or assumptions) to fill in the gaps. Then test, measure, adjust. Rinse and repeat. Forever.

Don't just look at the numbers. Talk to your customers. The ones who bought and especially the ones who didn't. Understanding the why behind the numbers is just as important as the numbers themselves.

Don't be afraid to raise your prices. If you're not regularly testing higher prices, you're leaving money on the table. You might be surprised at how elastic demand really is, but you will know only if you test it.

Competitive Advantage

Your pricing strategy can be a powerful differentiator. In a sea of per-seat pricing, maybe you offer unlimited seats but charge based on usage. Or in a market full of complex, usage-based pricing, maybe you offer simple, predictable flat-rate pricing.

Your goal isn't to be the cheapest. If no one knows you exist because you have no volume, you probably couldn't give this product away for free. Your sales goal at this point is to be familiar but different in a way that matters to your customers. Price is what you pay. Value is what you get. Make sure your customers understand the difference.

Every single startup and probably many incumbents say the same thing: We have the best product, most features, highest uptime, best support, strongest community, blah, blah, blah. We've all heard the script. So if everyone is saying the same thing, you screaming, "No, but really *we* are the best!" is probably not going to work.

Whatever price you choose, you need to be able to justify it. Can you clearly articulate the value you provide? Can you show how your solution saves time, increases revenue, or solves critical problems for your customers? If not, you've got some work to do.

Raise Prices

At some point, you're going to need to raise your prices. Maybe your costs have gone up. Maybe you've added new features. Maybe you've realized you were undercharging all along. Whatever the reason, price increases are a fact of life in the startup world.

Price increases are tricky and are not something I'm going to go into here. I will say you need to be mindful of revenue expansion, growth, average revenue per user, and all that. Also, if you are so lucky to be having a conversation about a price increase that could impact your existing customers, it means you have customers, so you are on the next chapter of your journey. High fives.

If you are raising prices because you have a few customers and the price doesn't work, there is no strategy here. Grandfather in existing customers, at least for a while.

Finally

The right price is the one that allows you to sustainably deliver value to your customers while building a business on its way into profitability.

There's no magic calculator; your perfect price doesn't exist. It depends on so many variables: product, market, customers, timing, sales capability, customer type, wind direction... just get away from complex value-based pricing gymnastics. Start with a price you can stand behind, gather data, pray a little bit, and iterate as you learn anything. Do anything to reduce friction, build trust, and get to market. Simple and fair.

Earning the right to sell isn't about mastering sales techniques or the sales personas or the closer's playbook or killer decks. It's about showing up relentlessly, understanding your customer's problems better than they do, and being ruthlessly committed to solving them. You're not here to close deals: You're here to prove, one customer at a time, that what you've built deserves a place in the world.

You're looking for the tiniest cracks in the market, the smallest openings that might, just might, give you a moment of attention. It's about doing the right things relentlessly, but since you don't know the right things yet, you have to do everything. I know. It's exhausting. So let's wrap with some encouragement.

A good product at a decent price will always beat a perfect product that never sees the light of day. Get out there, start selling, and let the market do its job of teaching you what your product is really worth.

EARN IT

Set a price that makes the offer impossible to reject.

Not because of the low price but because of the compelling value you offer. You can change the price tomorrow, but you can't keep waiting to set a price.

13

EARN THE RIGHT
TO (NOT) PIVOT

THE SILENCE can be deafening when you've done everything right—or at least you think you have—but still nothing seems to land. You've been diligent. Cold emails. Social posts. Reddit replies. You're probably running some ads out of desperation. And yet, the volume just isn't there.

Those first customers are the hardest to get. For everyone. It takes time before the wind shifts and inbound leads start happening. Absolutely every fucking thing takes longer than expected, even when you knew it would. But you can't stop yourself from wondering, "Could our cold emails get more traction? Could we see a few more leads? What are we missing?" In the silence, something is speaking. There's a message there, but the signal is so weak you might not hear it. Or it just might not be the signal you want to hear.

Every single founder has this moment of absolute frustration. It fucks with your head. It makes it really hard to focus and persevere. The tape loop you're running says, "What's the point? I'm doing all this work for nobody." You have definitely entered your "Do I need to blow it all up?" phase. You can't stop asking, "Is this the wrong product? The wrong market? Should I pivot? What would that even look like? Am I out of time? Where did I go wrong?"

This is when many founders press the "I built it wrong" pivot button. Very likely it's too early to make that call. And pivoting is not an escape route for running away from problems. Founders get this far only by being resilient. Now is the time to remember you *are* a founder. You need to accept there will be monstrous moments of despair you have to endure, alone. But you know now that your job is to get up, shut up, and work out a way to survive.

Successful pivots result from making strategic, informed decisions, not giving in to gut reactions. So step away from the pivot panic button. In this chapter, I want you to think about where you stand so you can get better at making good, fast, data-informed decisions, whether they result in pivoting, iterating, or finding another, better way forward.

I'm going to say it one last time: Clock speed rules. Success comes from how quickly you release, learn, iterate, rerelease. That's what you are in control of. Everything else outside of that is largely not in your control. It's a fact: The fastest team to learn wins. So in this moment of deep doubt and frustration, take a big breath, say a small prayer, and get to work figuring out "How the fuck are we going to get out of this hole?"

Rather than fixating on a pivot as your best hope, focus on the messages the market may be sending. Sometimes market sensing can point the way. Shopify, for instance, started as a snowboard store. They built a system to manage their inventory and then realized the system, not snowboards, was their real product. Was that a mistake, a pivot, or an iteration? No matter. Shopify wouldn't exist if it hadn't first been a snowboard store picking up on some serious market vibes.

The Dip

Before we talk about pivoting, we need to talk about something that hits almost every founder but rarely gets discussed: The Dip. It's not burnout and it's not procrastination. The Dip is that brutal period between momentum and traction—when your initial adrenaline has burned out, but reality hasn't caught up. The results of your work aren't coming in fast enough to maintain excitement.

You're doing everything mostly right, but nothing seems to be moving forward. Small tasks feel massive, and there's a total lack of energy coming back at you. You show up, do the work, and still feel like you're punching concrete. Every. Single. Day.

Here's where it gets really tricky. How do you know if you're in The Dip or if the market is trying to tell you something? Is this a traction delay or a market signaling problem? The answer determines everything. A traction issue needs grit; you grow through it. A market issue needs humility; you adapt, pivot, or rethink.

Most founders get this wrong because both feel the same in the moment. The silence. The lack of momentum. The questioning everything. But they require completely opposite responses. If it's The Dip, doubling down on your current path is exactly right. If it's market feedback, doubling down is exactly wrong.

Entrepreneur and investor Ben Horowitz calls it "The Struggle," where everything feels like it's on the line, and you're constantly tested to hold on when everything in you is whispering to let it go. PayPal co-founder Peter Thiel frames it differently: Building something from zero to one is always unique and lonely because there's no roadmap. A perpetual dip.

The mindfuck is that The Dip can actually be a good sign. You've survived long enough to meet it, and that's a milestone most don't make. Not all founders who survive experience The Dip, and not all who experience The Dip survive.

Your brain is literally working against you. That initial dopamine rush of having all the answers, feeling in control, putting in the high-performance hours—that was rocket fuel. It created the initial launch but was never meant to power the whole journey.

The Dip happens when that dopamine falls away, but you haven't yet built the muscle memory that makes this new reality feel normal. You're caught between what was and what will be. One more time: You're caught between what was and what will be.

Everything feels harder than it should. You're going through the motions, mechanically executing tasks. The small wins don't have the same impact. You're questioning everything.

The Dip shows small signs of life, occasional customer wins, positive feedback, small victories that just aren't coming fast enough. Market problems show consistent resistance. Prospects understand your solution but still don't want it, conversations die after demos, and you keep hearing the same objections.

The easy advice would be to find your center, rediscover what excited you at the beginning, take a break, go for a run, eat more berries. Cool. Sure. If that's all it took, it wouldn't be a dip. It would be a divot between having a bad day and eating some berries.

Instead, start with these four moves.

1. Change your success metrics. (Secretly) adjust the expectations of what you can achieve. Clean your desk, have one call, send four emails, walk for fifteen minutes. Whatever it takes. Humble yourself with some achievable metrics. Break the pattern.

2. Insert something new into your routine. Make a tangible change that creates some tiny bit of forward momentum. Set aside a power hour of emails first thing, write tomorrow's battle plan before bed, block your calendar so you have some peace. The actual new thing doesn't matter; the point is to disrupt your current shitty pattern and create a new one.

3. Get back in traffic. Most founders in The Dip isolate. It's the worst thing you can do. Go to a startup meetup, even if you hate the idea before you even arrive. Just do something.

4. Embrace that wartime CEO mindset. As Horowitz says, wartime CEOs can't afford to waver. They take the hard steps with conviction, they do the work, they do not fall, and they win.

The Dip isn't something you overcome—you have to go through it. Every founder who's built something meaningful has gone through it; most go through it multiple times. This isn't about who's smarter or works harder. It's about who accepts The Dip as part of the journey rather than fighting it as an obstacle.

So before you pivot, get brutally honest with yourself: Is this really a failed strategy or are you just in The Dip? The Dip is testing your commitment to your vision and your commitment to not fail. How badly do you want this?

Data. Again.

You've got problems, sure. But what you really have is data. You're probably just not using it for anything other than getting depressed. I'm not going to make another speech on observability, but I am pretty confident that even if you read chapter 6, even if you agreed on principle, you don't have a good window into what's going on. You didn't invest in observability because bug fixes and that one killer feature took priority. It's okay, everyone does it.

But let's talk about how founders commonly misunderstand whatever bad data they do have, if only from a few users and a few bits. It often comes from not understanding that acquisition, conversion, and retention are totally connected but also totally isolated moments with very different objectives. Too many founders attribute lack of conversion to their product. Usually that is a false assumption. If you are not getting people into your product, how can your product be the problem?

So let's walk everything back for a second. Think about some activities you are probably using to drive conversions and how you are interpreting the data.

- You sent cold emails, but no one clicked. That's not your product; that's a bad email. Maybe it was a great email, but it went to the junk folder if you didn't warm them up. That's bad infrastructure.

- People clicked but didn't convert. That's not a bad email; that's a bad website.

- People clicked, a few started onboarding, then left. That's not a bad product; that's bad onboarding.

- You ran ads, but no one clicked. It's not the product; it's the ad.

- Some people clicked, but no one converted. That's not the ad; that's the website.

- You ran ads and sent emails, but you targeted the wrong audience. That's not the ads, the emails, the website, the onboarding, or the product; that's the wrong market.

You see what I'm getting at here? The problem is not the tool or the tactic. It's you. You have data to guide you; you're just not listening or market sensing. Before you panic and pivot, the key is to isolate each stage of the funnel and analyze it independently. Your product can be judged based only on the experience of actual users who complete that transaction. Everything else is about the journey to get there. Before you start tweaking and freaking, make sure you are solving the right problem-causing crickets.

Effort Is Good

Before you do anything drastic, let's break down every step between meeting a user and their completing a transaction. At each touchpoint, define the objective and how much time it takes. This is likely your third or fourth time doing this evaluation, but by now you have some early signals of where the friction might be. Your mindset has likely shifted from a purely product focus to sales, and your approach to unpacking these steps may also have matured.

I know we are talking about the golden handshake again and user delight, but this is within the context of the entire value chain, every step of the way, going back five steps before they even find out you exist.

You've got to know the following:

- How long does it take a user to get their first taste of value (delight) after landing on your website?
- How many steps or clicks or things got in the way?
- What if the user came to your site and could click Start Now? What if they could actually do something, make something, see something before committing to your paywall trial? Might that help deselect the explorers but give value to the buyers?
- What's the effort to the user at each step compared to the value they're seeing for taking that step?
- How long does it take (in seconds or minutes), and how might you accelerate that?

Then just to up the challenge you're facing, don't forget the merit of the *right amount of friction*. In large part, I agree with the narrative supporting frictionless experiences and single-click solutions, but a little effort is a good thing. Appreciation and delight can often come from us putting in the work, so don't rob your user of the satisfaction of achieving something (let them experience the joy of Earning the Right!).

How much can you streamline and simplify while still delivering that aha moment? Don't make it so easy that they just don't care.

If everything is your fault, then everything is within your power to fix, **which should feel oddly liberating.**

The First Pivot Is Mental

All founders excel at making assumptions and jumping to conclusions, and rightly so. We have trained ourselves to have all the answers. So here's a bold assumption. Founders will fall into one of two groups:

1. They assume the product is off or the market is wrong.
2. They know the product is epic if only "people would give it a chance."

And here's my conclusion. Whether you're in the first or second group, you have to make a shift. That shift is you.

Remember, we're well into the founder's "it's all your fault" playbook. Sometimes things take longer than expected. Sometimes you are right about everything, but the market moved. Sometimes you are right about everything but just haven't yet found your voice. If everything is your fault, then everything is within your power to fix, which should feel oddly liberating.

Here's a mental (and operational) pivot worth making. You probably still have an engineer working on your product, the one that no one is using, toiling away on all the shit you dumped to post launch/fast follow. Now might be a really smart time to convert that engineer into *sales* engineering.

Stop building. You don't need more features. You don't need a better UI. You need clarity. You need data. Above all, you need users. You need to understand what the hell is actually going on and no feature you are building is going to create new users for you.

Move your engineers from building new features to tracking user behavior to working on sales stuff. Or save that money and allocate it somewhere else. Invest in user experience. Forget about everything else, because with no users, nothing else you do matters.

When...

Sometimes it feels like nothing you do is going to fix it. That's when the p-word gets tempting. You have a new insight, see a new market, imagine a new idea. Let me be super clear. Pivot is a quasi-last resort. Don't pivot because you're frustrated. Pivot because the market signals are unmistakably telling you to.

Some of those strong signs are as follows:

The market is not biting, even when you are face-to-face with your atomic ICP.

You are out of reasonable options. You've run your playbook (and everybody else's), and it is just not resonating.

The data clearly suggests it. Sometimes, in your quest to solve one problem, you stumble into a bigger, more pressing, exciting, lucrative, appropriate, in-demand one. If the data is screaming at you to shift focus or if the data isn't screaming at you but you see a very clear space you didn't see before, it may be time to move.

If You Must, Pivot Smart

Pivot is not a requisite rite of passage. Although an overwhelmingly large number of success stories had a pivot in their journey, it doesn't mean you should be searching for one or that you should use that line ("we executed a hard pivot") as a badge of honor. Don't pivot because things are tough. Don't pivot because you're scared. Don't pivot because you see some shiny new thing that looks easier than what you're doing now. That said, if you're going to pivot. Pivot hard. Go all in.

Before making this kind of move, you must understand exactly why you're pivoting. Because this isn't a fix. It's a shift in your *entire* strategy. You better really know exactly what is broken, what has to change, and what you expect as a result. You need to be able to do exponentially better with version 2 than you did with version 1. How do you justify a pivot? Can you quantify and qualify what was broken or needs to change? Has the market shifted in unexpected ways? Or can you now see that you failed to validate the *problem* well enough in the beginning?

Pivoting, even when you don't have enough data, still has to be a data-first decision over an emotional one. To repeat: Don't pivot because you're frustrated or scared. Pivot because the data, honestly and objectively analyzed, tells you to. If the market is consistently telling you to shift, listen. But if it's just a hunch or a fear, hold the line. Run an experiment; don't burn version 1 to the ground just yet.

Pivoting may seem like your salvation, but it is very risky. You likely have less cash today than yesterday. You are taking everything you have done and saying, "We're changing that." Better understand the upside versus the risk. Ask yourself, "What's the worst thing that could happen if we pivot? What's the best outcome? What if we try to edge into a pivot? Can we test the theory first?" The temptation for first-time founders to pivot early, often for the worst reasons, is hard to resist. But the stakes are incredibly high—there is no second pivot. Get your ducks well in a row.

A true pivot isn't inherently a failure. It's a strategic realignment, reflective of a founder who knows when everything they have spent the last six months ago praying was true isn't true. It's scary for your reputation, your stakeholders, your team—and for you to admit it. But you own it.

When you decide to pivot, communication is key. Be transparent with your team about the reasons for the pivot and the new direction. Prepare a clear message for your investors that outlines the data-driven decision process. For customers, focus on how this change will better serve their needs. Remember, how you handle this transition can be just as important as the pivot itself.

Hurry up this time. Test the new direction quickly. Get something—anything—in front of customers as quickly as possible. Learn fast, iterate faster.

Hold the Line, Stay the Course

Most of the time, you shouldn't pivot at all. A premature pivot is the result of a messy founder who didn't do the work the first time. It may feel like the sexy move, the answer to all your problems, giving you new direction, new energy, new hope, new excitement, new everything. But almost every problem you are facing can be solved without burning the ship. Here are some things to practice when those initial customers aren't piling through the door.

Fight the fear. Fear is the most terrible advisor. If you're considering a pivot because you're afraid your current path isn't working, take a step back. Fear often masquerades as intuition, but it's not.

Expect change. Don't pivot because things aren't going exactly as planned. Things never go as planned. If you pivot with every deviation from the plan, you'll be a whirling dervish, never settling long enough to gain traction.

Resist shiny objects. Don't pivot because you think you see a giant new opportunity. The grass always looks greener on the other side (it's usually not). Every market, every product has its challenges. A potential move may look easier from the outside but looks are nearly always deceiving.

Avoid false comparisons. Some founders excel at hiding how awful and terrible everything is. So don't compare yourself to other founders or the cohabitants of your cool coworking space bragging about their amazingness. They are full of shit and probably have less money in the bank than you.

Dig in. Sometimes the bravest thing you can do is hold the line, grit your teeth, and push through. Every successful startup goes through periods where it looks like nothing is working. The ones that make it are the ones that figure out how to push through. They lift themselves out of the darkness and turn it into pure, positive, committed, forward-looking energy. Holding the line doesn't mean ignoring reality. It means having the courage to stay the course when things get tough, as long as the fundamental thesis of your business, your right to exist, still holds true.

In its early days, Amazon faced immense pressure and damning criticism. Many called it "Amazon.bomb" during the dotcom bust. But Jeff Bezos held the line, focusing on long-term vision over short-term profits. This persistence eventually paid off, turning Amazon into the e-commerce giant we know today.

Evolution. It's a Thing.

What if, instead of thinking in terms of pivots as your next best or only option, you adopted a mindset of continuous iteration?

Think about it. Every piece of feedback, every data point, every user interaction provides an opportunity to make small, valuable improvements. What if the answer you are looking for is evolution, not revolution? You can be responsive to market needs without losing sight of your core vision. You can be agile, not erratic. You can commit to making constant, incremental improvements rather than dramatic, potentially disruptive—or even self-destructive—changes.

Continuous iteration serves as a middle ground between holding the line and pivoting.

Holding the line is the status quo with occasional small changes. It comes with a low level of risk and maintains the core vision.

A *pivot* is a major change in strategy and tactics. It is high risk and represents a significant shift in focus and vision.

Continuous iteration requires small, frequent adjustments. It offers minimal risk and brings flexibility to executing the core vision.

If we go back to the bedrock truth that everything comes down to you, founder, then it's always better to know the full range of available options. There are more choices than the pivot to revive your company.

Hard Calls

Okay, so the chapter title is misleading. This was never about pivoting or not pivoting. It's about earning the right to make hard calls of all sorts to keep going.

This comes back around to you as the founder. Once you've gotten to launch, your work as a leader keeps asking more of you. Step up. Be able to say you have done rigorous data analysis. Show you have deep market understanding. Act with the humility to undergo honest self-assessment. Prove you have earned the right to make decisions. Stay the course or make a significant change. Now is the time to prove you've built the muscle to make tough decisions and to execute on them effectively.

You're not going to be right all the time. But at each critical juncture, are you willing to confront reality, admit when things aren't working, and have the courage to make changes when necessary?

Trust your data. Trust your honed instincts (when they're backed by evidence). And above all, keep moving forward. The path is crazy. It probably doubles back on itself while the destination remains the same. Build a product people actually want, need, and will pay for.

EARN IT

Really, deeply know that what you're doing is right. Keep fighting for what you believe.

14

EARN THE RIGHT TO AI, PART 2

Chapter 2 focused on why AI is everyone's superpower. You understand by now an important distinction, that AI is an accelerator, not a shortcut. I hope I've convinced you that your real edge will always lie in understanding your market and problem better than anyone else. If you really get that, then you've got the right to think about AI's application inside of your organization and your technology stack.

This chapter focuses on how to harness this edge and deploy AI to maximize the impact for you. How should you use AI to scale your capabilities and abilities, to iterate faster, and to execute at an unprecedented level? The goal is simple: Make AI your strategic partner, not a tagline, not an .ai domain name. The goal is to make smarter decisions faster, move at lightning speed, and get more done for less.

Everything hinges on one truth: AI is only as good as the foundation you've built for it. If your startup's base is weak,

AI will accelerate your failure. If your foundation is strong, AI will exponentially propel your journey.

The New Startup Playbook

If you're a nontechnical founder, you now have a non-secret weapon. Probably the most notable adjustment for founders is that the old startup playbook required you to have a technical cofounder just to have a shot. AI has changed but not completely removed that barrier. AI can make it possible for you to at least get through the prototype stage without a technical cofounder. But AI is not designing, writing, running, and innovating your technical delivery. So while you no longer must have a technical cofounder on day one (though it would be better to have one), you can at least get started without one.

What AI does exceptionally well is allow you to prototype, validate, and iterate at a speed that was unthinkable just a few years ago. You can test your idea in days, not months, and then make informed pivots. Until you find the right person, AI can be a quasi, -ish, kinda technical cofounder to help you bring your product to life. Whatever that means.

Good Data Is Your Foundation

The foundation for using AI effectively is clean, well-organized data. That's it. AI thrives on structure and patterns. If your data is scattered or unstructured, AI won't be able to provide meaningful insights or results. Let me repeat: AI will amplify your chaos if your shit is just awful or clarify vast amounts of data if you've got your shit together.

Think about data like you think about your code base. If a human can't make sense of it, AI won't either. As you build, be guided by these questions to create a baseline for an AI-ready solution:

Can you organize your data into clear categories or tables?
Are there consistent patterns or formats in your data?
Can you easily link different pieces of data together?
Is your data clean and free from errors or inconsistencies?

Most founders skip this unsexy but critical step of managing their data. They want to jump straight to the output. All they want to do is build a product. Don't. If you remember your job is to build a solution that solves a problem, you must do the work that will get you there faster. Good data is the fuel that powers AI. The cleaner and more structured your data is, the more powerful and accurate your AI can be. The quality of your data determines the ceiling of what's possible with AI. I'm saying it one more time for luck: Organize your data well, and you've set yourself up to leverage AI in unimaginable ways.

The Real How

We know this much about new technology: It's going to move fast, and it will probably go places we didn't anticipate. So what follows isn't intended to be a foolproof plan for how you engage AI. But if you haven't given much thought to AI's potential, here are some aspects worth considering.

Your Copilot

AI isn't just a tool; it can be your strategic copilot. It forces you to articulate, clarify, and refine your thinking. The act of writing down your thoughts and prompting AI to engage with them is a game-changer. Verbalizing a problem is often 99 percent of the journey to a solution. Even if AI's responses aren't perfect, they propel you forward. They trigger insights, validate or challenge your assumptions, and make your thinking sharper. Imagine being able to ask in secret, from the privacy of your basement, for an interrogation of the idea. Imagine asking it to ask you questions to help you flesh out the idea. Imagine asking it to help you better refine or articulate your position.

Your job is to engage in this conversation relentlessly. The more questions you ask, the more you write and explain, the clearer your own strategy becomes. AI creates a space for exploration and ideation to hone your thoughts, iterate faster, and sharpen your idea.

Research on Steroids

AI transforms how you understand your market. It knows your market better than any research you can find. It can analyze competitors, track trends, dig deep into customer behavior. It's a data scientist and researcher at your disposal. Kinda. AI will give you data, not insight. It's still your job to interpret, prioritize, and act on it. The real magic will always be you, seeing the signals, combining the breadth of AI with your true and deep market understanding.

Rapid Prototyping and Validation

From idea to prototype at warp speed. Generate landing pages, create functional product mockups, or automate basic processes. You can go from idea to feedback from prospects in real time at almost zero cost and continue to iterate and improve as the insights arrive. AI cannot answer if this is a product the market actually wants. It might have a view, but it can enable this underlying process of discovery exponentially faster.

One more time: AI is an accelerant for learning, not just a productivity hack. Fastest to learn wins. Every time.

Personalization at Scale

Possibly the most exciting impact comes from delivering personalized experiences at scale. The ability to tailor content, automate engagement, analyze customer data, and deliver this snowflake-based response is epic. Imagine being able to tell a customer about a feature they haven't used and why it would be great for *them* or the impact it could have on *them* using their data... seamlessly.

I hate how many waivers I am writing, but don't mistake automation for connection. While AI might enable personalization, it will always be your understanding of your customers that makes connection meaningful. AI does not replace your personal touch, doing those unscalable things that set you apart at the early stage.

Assistants Versus Agents

The two main flavors of AI you'll be dealing with are assistants and agents. This isn't semantics; these are choices you'll make about how AI functions within your solution and business.

AI assistants help or augment but don't execute or make decisions. You're still the boss.

In customer support, for example, an AI assistant might analyze incoming messages and suggest relevant responses, but you decide which to use or how to modify them. In product development, an AI assistant might analyze user feedback and suggest potential new features, but you decide which ideas to pursue and how to implement them.

AI agents are the autonomous workers that can make decisions, execute tasks, and even interact with users or other systems on their own. This is where AI becomes a core part of your product, not just a tool you use internally. In customer support, the AI agents could directly interact with customers, answering queries without human intervention and deciding when to escalate issues to human support. In product development, they could automatically A/B test different features, analyze the results, and implement the best-performing versions without human intervention.

If you are just setting out, start with AI assistants. They can speed up routine tasks, do that useful analysis, test content, ideate product features, all with your final approval. As you validate and learn, start deploying AI agents for repetitive, scalable tasks such as customer support and pricing optimization. The goal is augmentation, not replacement.

Here's a list of competencies AI offers that you should be broadly familiar with.

- Natural language processing: Your language expert. Use it for automating customer interactions, content creation, and market research at scale.

- Computer vision: Your visual analyst. Essential if your startup deals with images or video in any way.

- Predictive analytics: Your fortune teller. Apply this to sales forecasting, churn prediction, and trend analysis.

- Generative AI: Your creative collaborator. Leverage it for design, content creation, and product development ideation.

- Reinforcement learning: Your optimization specialist. Perfect for solving complex problems such as dynamic pricing or creating personalized user experiences.

Everything hinges on one truth: **AI is only as good as the foundation you've built for it.**

Relax. You don't have to become an expert in all of these. But it is important to understand what they can do for your business. This is what I recommend you do with AI right now if this is all new to you:

- Do a brain dump. Take a walk and record everything you know about your startup idea, market, and plans. Don't filter—just let it flow. Puke it all out.

- Collect. Add this recording to any other relevant documents, research, or ideas you have.

- Upload. Use an AI tool that allows you to upload this information and then query it.

- Start querying. Ask this AI a bunch of questions about your startup: "What are we? What problem are we solving? What's our market? How might we enter the market? What's our 10x feature? What should we call ourselves? Should we do this? How do we work out market size? Where are the core challenges? Where should we start?" Just start asking. The answers may surprise you.

- Iterate and expand. Keep adding to this knowledge base as you learn more. Use it to organize your thoughts, generate ideas, and even draft documents. All of this is coming from *your* knowledge of *your* idea. You're using AI to edit, augment, expand, and ideate, *not* to do the thinking for you.

Remember, mastering AI is a learning process. As you get better with it, you get better with it. But you have to get started in order to get better.

Prompt Engineering

The secret sauce in AI isn't tech knowledge, it's mastering prompts. Learning how to give AI instructions is how you maximize its potential.

The more specific and detailed your prompts, the better the output. Use AI to refine your own prompts, to help you draft better questions, to improve how you talk to AI. That's the meta-game, and it's one you should learn to play.

Think of it like this: If you walked into a restaurant and just said "food," you'd get whatever the chef felt like making. But if you say, "I want a spicy Thai dish with chicken, extra veggies, and a coconut milk base, served in a deep glass bowl," you'll get exactly what you want.

Prompt engineering is about creating a structured conversation, one that pushes you to articulate what you're trying to achieve. It's a tool for reflection, refinement, and, ultimately, better execution.

Betting on the Unknown

What's coming?

We don't know exactly how AI will evolve, but we know three things for certain:

1. It's going to get exponentially better.
2. It's going to get exponentially faster.
3. It's going to get exponentially cheaper.

If your startup strategy hinges on AI not improving or relies on static capabilities, you're already dead. You have to bank on AI's relentless advancement. We already saw how this worked: Internet speeds increased, storage got cheaper, smartphone tech grew. In the early days, it's easy to bet against what we don't know, but betting against technology getting better is always a losing game.

So build with flexibility, ready to harness whatever comes. Part of staying curious and agile is always thinking about how your solution can ride the next wave of innovation.

It is still a universal truth that your systems should be designed to adapt, your strategy prepared to pivot, and your mindset ready to capitalize. Always be ready.

Your Force Multiplier

AI isn't a safety net; it's a springboard. It won't save a failing product, but it can help you work out why it's failing, refine, iterate, and explore, and amplify what you're doing right. If you've done the work, if you've truly earned the right to scale, AI is your ally, not your competition, not your cheat code.

The thing about earned rights is that they're not permanent. You have to keep earning them. The market shifts. Technology evolves. Customer needs change. Your right to win has to be re-earned every single day.

So keep learning, keep experimenting, keep pushing the boundaries because the founders who win won't be the ones who used AI best today. They'll be the ones who kept earning the right to use it better tomorrow.

EARN IT

This advice about AI isn't to suggest you automate everything or become an expert overnight. I'm advocating that you harness AI's power to free your mental space to do the work that really matters. Write down what that might look like. Name the actual tasks.

The most important job is the one only you can do. Understand your customers in order to solve their very real problem—that's it.

15

EARN THE RIGHT
TO TAKE A VACATION

DEAR FOUNDER,

We started on this journey as pirates. Both of us. We hustled, struggled, doubted, got way frustrated, cussed a lot. And yet we're still standing. We've come a long way, and in the process, we've earned the right to show our other side, as romantics. So, yes, this is my love letter to you, dear founder.

Before we go any further, I have something to confess. Everything I've put into this book is an opinion: a collection of ideas to help you think about thinking. I've asked you reasonable questions I expected you to know the answers to. And when you didn't, I hope I provided a path to help you find your answers. This is your journey, your way. By shouting encouragement and advice from the sidelines, I tried to mitigate some of the risks and disappointments you will most certainly face.

If after reading this book you feel a bit cleverer, readier, more founder-like, and at least a touch clearer on what it is you want to do, then I've done my job. Take a deep, full breath. Reflect on where you are and where you started out, specifically in these four areas.

Your problem: Chances are your understanding of the problem has evolved. Maybe it's deeper, maybe it's different, but most definitely you get by now what it means to really, truly know a problem.

Your solution: Your product today probably looks different from what you initially envisioned. Hundreds of tiny iterations all done before you wrote a line of code come from being willing to let the market help shape your offering.

Your market: Who are your actual customers today? Not the ones you imagined, but the ones who are actually going to get the most impact, the most value, and, most importantly, are actually going to be willing and able to buy your product. You know them.

Yourself as CEO: You're not the same person who started this journey. You've grown, you've learned, you've stumbled, you've stood back up, and you've gotten stronger. You're ready.

Remember in the beginning when I begged you *not* to raise money? When I told you that chasing investors was a fool's errand? That first you needed to focus on building something people actually want? It is my hope you are not that delusional dreamer anymore.

If you've done the work, you're no longer just another founder with a pitch deck and a prayer. You're a CEO who understands your market, who has data to back up your claims, who knows your customer. You've moved from selling a dream to offering a viable investment opportunity.

Maybe, just maybe, you're ready to raise money. Not because you need it to start, but because you need it to scale. Not because you're hoping someone else will validate your idea, but because you've already validated it yourself. You're not looking for cash; you're looking for a partner. Someone who can help you get to the next step on your journey, a journey you have already started.

So go take that meeting. Show them what you've built. Show them what you've learned. Show them the founder you've become, one who has earned the right to be taken seriously.

Be proud of how far you've come. But don't get complacent. You've earned the right to be here but not to *stay* here. The market doesn't care about your past achievements. It cares about the value you're creating right now and the value you'll create tomorrow.

So what's next? What's the next right you're going to earn?

Maybe it's the right to lead a larger team. To expand into new markets. The right to reshape your industry. To change the way people live or work. To leave a lasting impact. Maybe the reasons you started this journey are no longer the reasons you are excited to continue it.

So go out there and keep earning the right. Keep learning. Keep growing. Most importantly, keep building. Because the world needs what you're creating. It needs your vision, your grit, your relentless pursuit of better.

You got this. Show them what a real founder looks like.

Let's fucking go. Again.

Ad astra per aspera.

Your friend through whatever comes next,

JAMES

ACKNOWLEDGMENTS

LIKE EVERY startup, this book exists because of the people who believed in it, shaped it, and helped it find its market. Acknowledgments are an insufficient currency for thanks.

Every founder needs an epic chief technology officer (CTO). Someone who can hear their words, extract and architect the vision, prioritize what matters, and ship something worth building. Most founders judge progress by lines of code written. Second-time founders know that a great CTO is measured by lines of code they prevent from being written. Marilyn Anthony was my CTO. She turned my founder chaos into clarity by revealing my truth and my story in fewer words. She was a force multiplier in earning the right to share these lessons with you.

Every founder needs a cofounder who lets them dream without constraints, sees through their bullshit, keeps them on track, and who everyone knows is really running the show. That's my wife and kids. I married up.

Every founder needs a tribe of diverse people willing, wanting, and able to give feedback when it matters. That's my clients.

Every founder needs a market. A market they feel so strongly they can build into. A market that validates they're building something people want and will pay for. Where distribution comes before product. That's my more than 150,000 newsletter readers who helped me refine and clarify what people actually want to read, thoughtfully told to me via open rates!

Every founder needs those incredible people who make everything work behind the scenes, get none of the credit but deserve most of it. Bibiano, Alex, and Artur are the essential infrastructure that keeps everything running.

Every founder needs cheerleaders. This could have been a book about crochet, and it would have gotten the exact same feedback. Because sometimes what matters most are the people who believe in us unconditionally, not just our ideas. That's my parents.

And every founder needs villains. You know who you are. Thank you.

Finally, my thanks to the team at Page Two for helping bring this book to life. Like any good investor, they liked the market, liked the opportunity, saw the potential, and provided the resources to make it happen.

Thank you for helping me earn the right to write this book. Now it's time to help others earn their right to build something that matters.

NOTES

1. Let's Fucking Go

p. 22   *"a crisis is a terrible thing to waste"*: Jack Rosenthal, "A Terrible Thing to Waste," The New York Times, July 31, 2009, https://www.nytimes.com/2009/08/02/magazine/02FOB-onlanguage-t.html.

p. 30   *Stay humble, stay hungry, stay foolish*: Ailian Gan, "The Origins of 'Stay Hungry, Stay Foolish,'" Medium, January 17, 2017, https://medium.com/ailiangan/the-origins-of-stay-hungry-stay-foolish-5a4a8d626f2.

5. Earn the Right to Enter the Market

p. 76   *Red Ocean or Blue Ocean?*: W. Kim Chan and Renée Mauborgne, *Blue Ocean Strategy: How to Create Uncontested Market Space and Make the Competition Irrelevant* (Harvard Business Review Press, 2015).

6. Earn the Right to Avoid Chasing Product-Market Fit

p. 103   *Build a thing, get people to love that thing*: "Mark Zuckerberg Explains His Playbook for Building Threads, Facebook, and WhatsApp," posted July 31, 2024, by Startup Archive, YouTube, 1 min., 24 sec., https://www.youtube.com/watch?v=5_qvJfɪfiSA.

8. Earn the Right to Delight

p. 142   *users form an opinion in* milliseconds: Javier Bargas-Avila, "Users Love Simple and Familiar Designs—Why Websites Need to Make a Great First Impression," Google Research, August 29, 2012, https://research.google/blog/users-love-simple-and-familiar-designs-why-websites-need-to-make-a-great-first-impression.

p. 142   *a poor experience turns away 88 percent of users*: The Trillion Dollar UX Problem: A Comprehensive Guide to the ROI of UX (Amazon Web Services, n.d.), 8, https://s3.amazonaws.com/coach-courses-us/public/theuxschool/uploads/The_Trillion_Dollar_UX_Problem.pdf.

p. 142   *better checkout design increases conversions*: "49 Cart Abandonment Rate Statistics 2025," Baymard Institute, updated July 11, 2023, https://baymard.com/lists/cart-abandonment-rate.

p. 145   *62 percent of users expect you to anticipate their needs*: "What Are Customer Needs and The Strategy to Meet Them," *Salesforce India Blog*, October 18, 2023, https://www.salesforce.com/in/blog/what-are-customer-needs.

9. Earn the Right to Ship

p. 169   *LinkedIn cofounder Reid Hoffman said it best*: Reid Hoffman and Chris Yeh, *Blitzscaling: The Lightning-Fast Path to Building Massively Valuable Companies* (Crown Currency, 2018).

13. Earn the Right to (Not) Pivot

p. 223   *Entrepreneur and investor Ben Horowitz calls it "The Struggle"*: Ben Horowitz, *The Hard Thing About Hard Things: Building a Business When There Are No Easy Answers* (Harper Business, 2014).

p. 224   *PayPal co-founder Peter Thiel frames it differently*: Peter Thiel with Blake Masters, *Zero to One: Notes on Startups, or How to Build the Future* (Crown Currency, 2014).

p. 225   *wartime CEOs can't afford to waver*: Horowitz, *The Hard Thing*.

p. 234   *Many called it "Amazon.bomb"*: Jacqueline Doherty, "Amazon.bomb," *Barron's*, May 31, 1999, barrons.com/articles/SB927932262753284707.

PHOTO: DANA HANLEY

ABOUT THE AUTHOR

JAMES SINCLAIR is the founder's founder. A serial entrepreneur with multiple exits who thrives in the chaos of early-stage startups. Where nothing is certain, James is the guy they call to help founders transform ideas into something customers actually want to buy.

He's guided ventures through Y Combinator and TechStars, worked with founders from Uber, Intel, and Meta, and built a reputation as the go-to strategist for turning dreams into viable, market-ready businesses.

His weekly newsletter reaches 150,000 founders, who read his candid, actionable insights to navigate the brutal realities of starting a startup.

James has led innovation projects across both private and public sectors, most recently spearheading rapid innovation initiatives at SAP for giants like LinkedIn, Google, and Citi.

His mission is simple: Arm first-time founders with no-fluff strategies to stop building nonsense and start building businesses that win.

Learn more at startuptoscaleup.com.

Good luck, wherever this journey takes you.
Keep me in the loop.

You are welcome to email me. I read and respond to most messages, except the crazies:
james@startuptoscaleup.com

Connect with me on LinkedIn:
linkedin.com/in/jdsinclair

Find additional resources, frameworks, and other helpful information on my website:
startuptoscaleup.com

LFG.